STEM Educ

MW01088808

An accessible text that assumes no prior knowledge, this book is grounded in the realization that "STEM" and "STEM Education" have not yet evolved into fully-coherent fields of study, and fills this gap by offering an original model and strategy for developing coherences in a way that both honors the integrity of each of STEM's constituent disciplines and explores the ways they can amplify one another when used together to address complex contemporary issues. This book demonstrates how STEM can and should be understood as more than a collection of disciplines; it is a transdisciplinary, possibility-rich domain that is much more than the sum of its parts. Building on the actual work of scientists, engineers, and other professionals, the authors disrupt preconceptions about STEM domains, and provide the tools and evidence-based approaches to create new possibilities for all learners. Covering historical influences, theoretical frameworks, and current debates and challenges, this book positions teachers and students as agents of change. Each chapter features In Brief openers to introduce the topic; Opening Anecdotes to reflect the chapter's key themes; Sidebars to put core principles in context; Consolidating Key Points activities to summarize and highlight important details; and Challenges to build upon and extend topics explored in the chapter from different angles.

Brent Davis is a Werklund Research Professor in the Werklund School of Education, University of Calgary, Canada.

Krista Francis is Assistant Professor of STEM Education in the Werklund School of Education at the University of Calgary, Canada.

Sharon Friesen is Professor of Mathematics Education in the Werklund School of Education at the University of Calgary, Canada.

STEM Education by Design

Opening Horizons of Possibility

Brent Davis | Krista Francis | Sharon Friesen
University of Calgary

Routledge
Taylor & Francis Group

NEW YORK AND LONDON

First published 2019
by Routledge
52 Vanderbilt Avenue, New York, NY 10017

and by Routledge
2 Park Square, Milton Park, Abingdon, Oxon, OX14 4RN

Routledge is an imprint of the Taylor & Francis Group, an informa business

© 2019 Taylor & Francis

The right of Brent Davis, Krista Francis, and Sharon Friesen to be identified as authors
of this work has been asserted by them in accordance with sections 77 and 78 of the
Copyright, Designs and Patents Act 1988.

All rights reserved. No part of this book may be reprinted or reproduced or utilised in any
form or by any electronic, mechanical, or other means, now known or hereafter invented,
including photocopying and recording, or in any information storage or retrieval system,
without permission in writing from the publishers.

Trademark notice: Product or corporate names may be trademarks or registered trademarks, and are used only for identification and explanation without intent to infringe.

Library of Congress Cataloging-in-Publication Data
Names: Davis, Brent, author. | Francis, Krista, author. | Friesen, Sharon, author.
Title: STEM education by design : opening horizons of possibility / Brent Davis, Krista
Francis, and Sharon Friesen.
Description: New York : Routledge, 2019 |
Includes bibliographical references.
Identifiers: LCCN 2018061620| ISBN 9780367111571 (hardback) |
ISBN 9780367111632 (pbk.) | ISBN 9780429025143 (ebook)
Subjects: LCSH: Science--Study and teaching. | Technology--Study and teaching. |
Engineering--Study and teaching. | Mathematics--Study and teaching. | Interdisciplinary
approach in education.
Classification: LCC Q183.3.A1 D38 2019 | DDC 507.1/073--dc23
LC record available at https://lccn.loc.gov/2018061620

Typeset in Palatino and Arial
by Brent Davis

Publisher's Note: This book has been prepared from camera-ready copy provided by the
authors.

Contents

Chapter 1

STEM

disciplinarity   transdisciplinating

IN BRIEF

Calls for enhanced STEM **education** are becoming more frequent and more urgent. But they're not all the same. Some are framed in terms of *more*, others in terms of *different*.

For centuries, public schooling has been organized around sharp distinctions among disciplines – an approach that might be limiting **learning** rather than enabling it.

Conceptions of "good **teaching**" are derived in large part from cultural beliefs about the purposes of education. Two very different views on teaching and education are examined.

STEM Challenges

Michael seemed to have been born with a love of dinosaurs. Through his preschool years, he was drawn to any and all dinosaur-related information. The zoo's dinosaur park was one of his favorite places, and he had memorized every part. Trips to the library resulted in heavy bags of dinosaur picture books. By the time he entered Kindergarten he was able use appropriate scientific terms to communicate his knowledge. For example, he could explain the differences between a pteranodon and a pterodactyl, a stegosaurus and an anklosaurus, a triceratops and a styracosaurus. He could classify species as omnivores, carnivores, or herbivores. He knew about the environments in which they lived, how they raised their young, and so on.

Yet, Michael's first Kindergarten report card gave no indication of these or any other interests or capabilities. Instead it provided an accounting of things he couldn't do. For instance, he couldn't tie his shoes (notwithstanding that he had never needed to do so; his shoes had Velcro closures). He didn't know how to write all his letters. And so on. The checklist report card, based on an outcome-driven curriculum, detailed Michael's inadequacies rather than his strengths – and the resulting list of shortfalls was so extensive that Mr. Richards couldn't help but voice his worry that Michael might not be able to catch up to his peers.

Michael's encounters with an ends-oriented, checklist-based education didn't end there. It popped up regularly with reports of unmastered skills or unmemorized facts – or, most frustratingly, as simply a lack of ability, as happened with his Grade 10 mathematics. He was regularly failing exams. Wanting to be of assistance, his mother began to review his test papers, hoping to identify misunderstandings of concepts. But she found the opposite, as it was quickly evident that he understood the mathematics but was prone to making simple calculation errors. That wasn't reflected in the grading, however. His teacher, Ms. Radler, gave marks only for right answers. On one test, Michael answered just one of four questions correctly, and so Ms. Radler assigned a score of 25%. The situation would have been very different had she given credit for a correct solution method. For example, if the method had been allotted 80% of the grade and the solution allotted 20%, Michael would have received a grade of 85% (= 80/80 for correct method + 5/20 for correct responses).

Michael's parents were thus unsurprised when, in parent–teacher interviews, Ms. Radler explained that Michael was "not very good at mathematics." From a checklist perspective on curriculum and a correct-answers perspective on grading, Ms. Radler seemed justified. From a mathematical understanding perspective, however, she was not. In fact, later that same year, Michael came third in his school on a mathematics contest, and his school was ranked in the top ten nationally. That is, far from being "not very good at mathematics," there were indications of a prodigious ability in the discipline.

Thankfully, that ability has since been recognized. By the third year of his undergraduate studies in electrical engineering, Michael was on the Dean's list. Later, in his master's program in bio-engineering, he contributed to designing and prototyping two innovative instruments. One measured stomach motility with a non-invasive pill that is swallowed; the other, called an "e-mosquito," was a wrist-watch-style device that measured blood sugar at regular intervals without the wearer feeling it. Michael is now extending his studies into medicine, so there seems good reason to expect even more substantial and innovative contributions.

Consolidating Key Points

Every year, Careercast.com ranks 200 mid-income careers, based on a range of qualities such as work environment, income, and job stability. Visit the site and look at the highest- and lowest-ranking careers. (You might also want to review the details they provide on their methodology.)

How does STEM Education figure into the picture? How long have the highest-ranking careers been around? How about the lowest-ranked careers? A major impetus for the first public schools in the 1700s and 1800s was to prepare children for the adult work world. Contrast career landscapes and schooling structures from then and now.

STEM Education

Science, Technology, Engineering, and Mathematics (STEM) Education is in the news. As reviewed in greater detail in the chapters that follow, it's being discussed at local, national, and international levels and across multiple agencies, many of which have no direct responsibility for schooling.

We're glad to see the growing interest. Like many, we see an improved STEM Education as vital. However, at the same time, we are frustrated by many of the assumptions and assertions that seem to float around in current discussions. To our ears, the message often seems to be about *more* and *better* STEM Education – that is, more courses, more hours, more rigorous outcomes, more accountability for teachers, and so on.

The episode recounted in this chapter's opening anecdote was selected to highlight this detail. We wholeheartedly agree that STEM Education should receive renewed attention, but we also believe that this attention should be formatted for today's world. Contemporary STEM Education tends to reflect decisions made centuries ago, especially around science and mathematics. Most of today's commonplace teaching methods, curriculum contents, classroom designs, and evaluation regimes arose in the 1700s and 1800s as educators and policy makers grappled with the complex task of designing a schooling system that was fitted to the emerging needs of a dramatically changing world. Industrialization, urbanization, democratization, capitalism, and other major cultural trends in the western world presented the need for literate and numerate citizens who could fill new social and economic roles.

Their decisions on standardized practices, curricula, classrooms, and examinations met the need. Western cultures and economies flourished, in no small part through the contributions of formal schooling. However, it's not clear that the educational decisions made a few hundred years ago are still appropriate. As we hope is evident in this chapter's opening anecdote, it often seems that some learners succeed *in spite of* and not *because of* their public schooling experiences.

Before we go any further, though, we should make one point clear. We have presented this anecdote to

Arguments for STEM Education are often framed in terms of economics. What does the economy need? How can we gain advantage? And so on.

We take a different perspective in this book. Here STEM Education is about opening learners' horizons of possibility and keeping them open as long as possible. It is not about directing students toward particular choices, but about affording them as much choice as possible. Lack of STEM knowledge can be limiting, and so quality STEM Education is a social justice issue.

many people, and many hearers and readers have inferred that the story represents a criticism of specific teachers. Our point, they concluded, is that Mr. Richards and Ms. Radler are simply "bad" educators.

That's not at all what we're saying. True, they did ignore Michael's interests and talents. True, they did pay more attention to what Michael didn't know than what he did know. But that's because, by the standards of a centuries-old educational system, they were actually *good* teachers. Mr. Richards and Ms. Radler were doing exactly the jobs they were hired to do. They attended to the sets of skills and collections of facts that curriculum developers had identified as vital, and their efforts were informed by key milestones and markers that psychologists and other researchers had identified as important in the development of "normal" children. Moreover, by all accounts, their classrooms were well managed and curricula were covered from start to finish.

Clearly, the way Michael was taught is an issue. But the more critical concern is the system in which that mode of teaching makes sense. And it's that matter that we seek to challenge in this book.

Stated differently, while we agree that an enhanced emphasis on STEM Education is appropriate, rather than thinking in terms of *more*, we believe the emphases should be on *different*. We look toward a model of schooling that is structured around what learners know and what they might do rather than what they don't know and can't do. We prefer to see learners as dynamic agents actively engaged with others and capable of making important contributions to a shared world, and not as deficient vessels to be filled, fixed, or completed.

We signal this notion of a different STEM Education in the subtitles of every chapter:

1 – **STEM** ((disciplines) transdisciplinating)
2 – **Learning** ((acquisition) participating)
3 – **Mathematics** ((calculation) modeling)
4 – **Technology** ((usage) designing)
5 – **Engineering** ((application) innovating)
6 – **Science** ((method) inquiring)
7 – **STEM Education** ((reception) contributing)

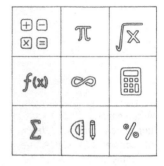

Collected above are some of the more prominent icons for "math" and "mathematics," based on an internet image search.

Which of them align with your understandings of the discipline? If you were required to select one (or to design one, if none of these works for you) to use in your own teaching, what would you choose?

Each pair of words in the subtitles is intended to flag a possible elaboration in the traditional emphases of public schooling. For example, the original aim of school mathematics was to prepare learners to operate in an industrialized, capitalist, and computerless world. Obviously, an emphasis on rapid and accurate calculation was appropriate. Unfortunately, however, that emphasis may have been too successful. As is evident in the imperative, "Do the math!", the words *calculation* and *mathematics* are often treated as synonyms. In Chapter 3, we thus propose a different frame for school math, one that is concerned with *modeling*. As we discuss in that chapter, this emphasis is not intended to replace calculation. Rather, we see it as a more expansive and encompassing notion, one that includes but transcends calculation. We believe it to be an emphasis that is better fitted to the learning needs of today's world.

Similar might be said of all the word pairings in the subtitles, and especially for the coupling of *disciplines* and *transdisciplinating* in this chapter. One of the major innovations of the Scientific Revolution was the movement toward clear delineation of disciplines. Researchers realized, for example, that investigations of living systems required specialized methods that weren't entirely the same as those used to study mechanical systems. This emphasis on disciplinarity is a critical element of scientific inquiry and has been a dominant theme in school science for centuries.

Some questions, however, don't lend themselves to discipline-based inquiry. Consider, for example, the sorts of societal and ecological worries that are currently prominent in the news, in politics, and in popular debate. These have been described as "wicked problems" – that is, problems that are difficult or impossible to solve because they are shifting forms. They defy efforts to define, categorize, or reduce. Multi-perspectival interpretations are needed to address them. Such are the two defining elements of transdisciplinarity: firstly, transdisciplinary efforts are focused on complex, real-world problems; secondly, these problems require the insights from more than one discipline (Choi & Pak, 2006).

The first recorded use of the word *technology* to refer to tools and tool use was in 1859, and the first recorded use of *high-tech* (as in "digital technologies") was in 1972. It's thus interesting to notice that most icons for technology focus on this much more recent notion.

How do the above images resonate with your understanding of the word?

Transdisciplinarity doesn't replace disciplinarity. They complement one another. We hope that all the chapters are read with that notion in mind. The point isn't that the emphases of traditional schooling are wrong for today's world; it's that they might have become inadequate and so formal education must evolve. It must elaborate its history without losing that history.

On that detail, notice that the each of the pairs of words in the chapter subtitles comprise a noun and a verb. The nouns point not just to prior needs, but to traditionalist educational sensibilities that focus on objectified facts, objectives of learning, and objective measures of achievement. The verbs in the chapter subtitles are intended to suggest a more open, flexible, adaptive attitude, one that is less about accumulation of established truths and more about engaging with/in an evolving world.

Consolidating Key Points

Icons are devices used to compress meaning. Because of that, icons can serve as a sort of "ink blot test" – that is, they offer windows into beliefs and assumptions. For instance, consider how you might assemble a STEM icon by choosing one element from each of the four boxes here. (An image search will generate many other alternatives if you don't like these choices.) Which icons "speak" to you? Which don't? Why? Do you find the disciplinary–transdisciplinary dyad useful for making choices and noting contrasts?

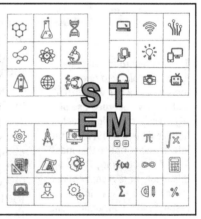

How we're hoping you'll use this book

We see this text as an extended *essay*, in the original sense of the word. Derived in the late 1400s from the Middle French *essai*, "trial, attempt," the word essay entered English as a verb that originally meant something like "to put to proof, test the mettle of" (*O.E.D.*, Weiner et al., 1993). As its noun form emerged, an essay was first understood as a sort of thought experiment, an effort to think through possibilities, an attempt to address evolving circumstances and emerging issues.

Thus, this book should be read as a set of suggestions or possibilities, not as a collection of assertions or claims. Our intention is to be provocative. We aim to spark conversation and debate by considering STEM Education in terms of historical influences, theoretical framings, and accumulated evidence.

On that count, we have attempted to be especially attentive to developments in the cognitive sciences – a transdisciplinary domain that brings together neuroscience, psychology, linguistics, education, and other disciplines around a shared interest in how humans learn. There have been many new insights into learning over the past century, and we have tried to incorporate some of those developments in the way this resource is structured. Resulting features (and why we've included them) are …

Engineering is probably the most poorly understood of the STEM disciplines, and part of the reason for that might be evident in the logos that pop up on an image search for "engineering logo." There's not a lot a range, and most of these examples zero in on mechanical artifacts.

Do any of these icons resonate with you? If so, why? If not, extend the search or design one of your own that you feel better reflects the field of engineering.

IN BRIEF – What people notice usually has more to do with what they know and expect than with what they don't know or don't expect. Each chapter thus begins with a sort of priming – that is, quick summaries of key themes to orient attentions.

OPENING ANECDOTE – Narratives that are based on experiences are engaged differently than fact-focused expositions. That's why we open each chapter by recounting an event that reflects key themes of the chapter, hoping that these accounts might trigger relevant memories from your own educational experiences.

CONSOLIDATING KEY POINTS – Humans have quite extraordinary capacities to remember, but very limited working memories. In practical terms, it's possible to know a lot, but still be easily overwhelmed by small amounts of new information. That's why we've inserted pauses after each section of the main text, offering activities and questions intended to highlight and consolidate important details.

SIDEBARS – One of the most effective ways to develop understanding of new principles is to rephrase and reframe them. The sidebars in each chapter are inserted for this reason. Each is intended as an invitation to reflect on key details from a slightly different angle.

CHALLENGES – We end the chapters with challenges that build on and extend the topics explored in the sidebars. Whereas the sidebars are more focused on *your learning*, the challenges are more concerned with *your teaching*. They are offered as opportunities to identify, analyze, apply, and rehearse topics in ways intended to help you prepare for the classroom.

To be clear, this book should not be read or assigned as a textbook. For us, such uses align with precisely the mentality that we hope might be interrupted. The broad goal is for you to participate actively, not to be a passive recipient.

Consolidating Key Points

At the end of the last century and into the first decade of this one, "21st-century skills" and "21st-century learning" became buzz phrases.

Most often, these notions were originally associated with digital technologies and interpersonal competencies, but their definitions have evolved. What else might the phrase entail for you? Do an internet search to see how others have modified and extended the ideas. To what extent do your and others' interpretations of "21st-century skills/learning" involve STEM disciplines? To what extent do you believe they should?

Nearing the end of this century's second decade, mentions of "21st century" are starting to feel a little dated. If you were tasked with coining a replacement phrase, what would you suggest?

Summing up

The world is changing. No one debates that point.

What is less obvious, however, is that pace of change is changing. It's accelerating.

Among the many upshots of the many accelerations that are now being experienced is the realization that the goals and purposes of traditional education – namely, to prepare children for their adult roles – is more and more difficult to manage. Whereas not long

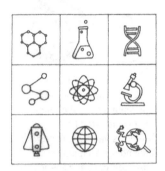

Science comprises many domains. For instance, high school graduates in North America will have studied topics in physics, chemistry, and biology – and, perhaps a few other branches.

Yet the most popular logos for science point mostly to chemistry. Why might that be?

Critique these logos. Do they resonate with your experience of science? Is that a good thing or a bad thing? Do they reflect the project of modern scientific research?

ago educators could predict with reasonable confidence what a learner would need upon graduation, that's just not the case any more as career landscapes change, as knowledge domains develop and intersect, as environmental contexts evolve, and so on.

STEM Education is not only a response to accelerating change, it is intended to contribute to that change. That is, STEM Education isn't about adding more math and science. It entails a dramatic rethinking of what schooling is all about.

Our suspicion is that most people agree that traditional schooling is no longer a good fit for today's cultural and ecological circumstances. The agreement has been especially obvious in the responses we've witnessed from people who've heard or read the narrative that opened this chapter. Overwhelmingly, initial reactions have revolved around how important it is for teachers to be attuned to students' interests and insights ... and that educators shouldn't be so obsessed with such skills as tying shoes and doing accurate calculations.

But, as already emphasized, that wasn't the point of the narrative. On the contrary, in fact, we regard shoe-tying and correct calculations as tremendously valuable competencies. We don't mean to suggest that such foci should be replaced, but that they should be elaborated. On that count, throughout this book we strive to sidestep a pervasive, insidious, and unproductive educational debate. We are not advocating for/ against a back-to-basics curriculum, just as we are not advocating for/against an education based on play and discovery. Rather, we argue for an educational conversation, one that is interested in expanding possibilities, for individuals and for society. For us, the emergence of broad interests in STEM Education affords an opportunity to think through how this might happen.

Why?

Partly because, as we explore in Chapter 2, the emergence of STEM Education affords a timely opportunity to expose and interrogate many of the assumptions about knowledge, learning, and teaching that hold current schooling practices in place.

Partly because, as is discussed in more detail in

Chapter 3, STEM Education's emphasis on real-world problems helps cut through the nonsense of the "Math Wars" that have been raging for nearly a half century.

Partly because, as is illustrated by Chapter 4's discussion of coding, STEM Education is forcing reconsiderations of what is "basic," what it means to be "literate," and how such constructs are tethered to time and location.

Partly because, as illustrated in Chapter 5's anecdote of middle school students innovating on catapult designs, STEM Education invites us to approach schooling from a perspective that learners are competent and always-innovating agents rather than deficient and passive receptacles.

Partly because, as explored in Chapter 6, scientific inquiry is more than step-following and rule-obeying. Rather, it is a mode of disciplined study that is rooted in and that amplifies the natural inquisitiveness that defines humanity.

That is, as we argue in Chapter 7, the STEM disciplines are humanities. They are about understanding ourselves, others, the worlds we share … and about participating mindfully.

This point is critical to us. It's a thought that is woven through every aspect of this book. And it's also the reason that it's about STEM Education rather than STEAM Education.

STEAM is an acronym that has been proposed by some who either are concerned that an amplified emphasis on STEM domains might further erode Arts programs in schools, or believe that STEM domains need the Arts to become more self-aware. We see at least three problems here. Firstly, the desire to insert an "A" seems to be anchored to a belief that there will always be a gap between STEM and the Arts – a line of thinking that leads to the conclusion that something *more* needs to be added (i.e., inserting an "A" into STEM) rather than considering the need to think in *different* terms (i.e., recognizing that STEM domains are humanities – rooted in human experience, fitted to human cognition and perception, oriented by human interests, etc.).

Secondly, squeezing a single "A" into the four letters

Two different visual metaphors for thinking about the relationships among sets of phenomena are illustrated here.

Above is an image used to signal non-overlapping sets. It's the sort of image associated with dichotomies and other radically separated forms.

Below is a nested image, used to flag subsets. Variations of this image appear frequently in this book. We use it to highlight that, when it comes to many educational issues, thinking in terms of "include but extend" is often more appropriate than "this or that."

of STEM seems to us to be a diminishment. Concealed in that "A" are diversities of interest and depths of expertise that are at least as broad and profound as the combined STEM realms.

Thirdly, there have been many recent events in which STEM-enabled tools and platforms have contributed significantly to social, political, cultural, and environmental challenges – or, perhaps more appropriately, crises. Around these pressing matters, a post hoc insertion of Arts into STEM might be construed as a deflection – a too-little-too-late attempt to duck the realization that unchecked STEM knowledge can be profoundly destructive.

To be clear on where we sit with the STEM/STEAM issue, we actively and passionately advocate for better developed Arts programs in schools. However, for the reasons just mentioned, we believe that stirring a dollop of "A" into the stew of "STEM" may signal regressive thinking while it actually diminishes both the Arts and the STEM domains.

Concisely, the move hints at continued *disciplinary siloing* rather than *transdisciplinary co-amplification* – that is, of *transdisciplinating* – which honors the specificity of all areas of human inquiry, but which calls for a blending of interest and expertise across issues confronting humanity and the more-than-human world.

STEM Challenges

1. As a young child, Michael (introduced in the chapter's opening anecdote) was quite knowledgeable about dinosaurs. He had an extended vocabulary; he understood scientific classification schemes; he knew what ate what; he knew which were born and which were hatched; he knew how different species raised their young, and so on. What were the processes that enabled his knowledge to deepen? Where did he develop this knowledge?

   Think about something that you're really good at. What makes you good at that something? What skills would be required to help someone else be good at what you're good at? How did you learn those skills? How long did it take you to become good? What sorts of teachers did you have, and how did they help you develop your skills? How did those teachers interact with you? What else in your environment helped or supported you?

   Now think about if what you are good at is related to what you learned in school, generally, and in your STEM-related school experiences, in particular?

Why do you suppose that is? Turn to the person beside you and discuss whether their "something they are good at" is STEM related. Or school related. Discuss why or why not?

2. In her 2011 TED talk, "My Mushroom Burial Suit" [https://www.ted.com/talks/jae_rhim_lee], artist Jae Rhim Lee explains her efforts to develop a more ecologically sound approach to dealing with corpses. Lee's mushroom suit is an exemplar of STEM innovation, one that is as notable for its challenge to entrenched beliefs as it is for its contribution to ecologically sound practices.

What sorts of issues are brought forward by this talk? Scientific issues? Technological issues? Engineering issues? Mathematical issues? Now go back through the dyads in the sidebars developed throughout this chapter. Use these sidebars to interpret Lee's approach for dealing with death. How is this a STEM thing? How is it not?

3. As authors, we engaged with the questions and prompts presented in this chapter's sidebars. Among the products of that engagement were the following pairs of icons for each STEM domain – which, for us, reflect the themes of the chapters announced in the subtitles.

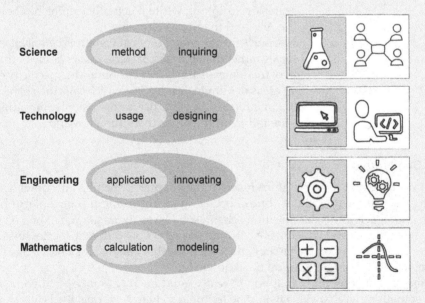

As noted in the first sidebar in this chapter, icons are intended to compress meaning and to signal key ideas. How do you think we did? Which resonate with you and which don't? Why might that be? What would you do differently?

Chapter 2

Learning

acquisition   participating

IN BRIEF

A century of intense research into cognition has revealed that many **educational** beliefs and practices are indefensible. Recent, evidence-based theories are reviewed.

Learning is popularly described in terms of physics (e.g., cause–effect mechanics). The evidence suggests frames based on biology (e.g., adaptive dynamics) are more defensible.

Teaching practices are often based on commonsensical "folk" theories that operate without challenge. To improve practice, teachers must be aware of the theories that infuse their work.

Learning Challenges

Teaching an innovative STEM Education course within the structures of the university has its challenges. The institution's administration is strongly budget conscious. Large class sizes translate to greater efficiencies and reduced costs. In addition to economic concerns, many of the structures of university courses still echo industrialized sensibilities around teaching and learning. Classrooms are frequently organized for a delivery-sort of teaching, positioning professors at the front of the room and placing students in forward-facing rows to receive their instructor's wisdom. For the teacher education program, classrooms are assigned by the university's central booking system based on one criteria: the number of  students in the course. In contrast to programs in medicine, engineering, science, and other domains – where labs, shared work, and other considerations specific to the disciplines often make for more generous and more carefully structured spaces – for teacher education, pedagogical strategies and student learning needs are not core considerations in the central system.

My STEM Education class in the Fall 2018 semester was located on the second floor of the Education Block, in a room that was classified to hold 50 students. The instructional space was clearly demarcated as the front of the classroom. The e-podium was planted just opposite the door. The center front was framed by a whiteboard and screen. The desks were arranged in tight, single-file rows, separated from one another by little more than a handspan. There was an extra whiteboard to the left, but it was impossible to access because the rows on the sides were pressed against the walls.

According to the institution's central booking standards, I had more space than necessary since there were only 36 pre-service teachers enrolled in the course. Yet, the room was almost impossible for my teaching and learning needs. For instance, the configuration made it difficult to adapt for collaborative small-group and large-group design spaces. More fundamentally, it made it nearly impossible for me to circulate. Once everyone was seated, with their winter coats and backpacks stowed wherever they could be tucked, I couldn't penetrate their space. With desks filling the room to capacity, there was minimal flexibility for reconfiguration.

Considerations with movement aside, just using different equipment posed immense challenges. A major component of the course was developed around assembling and programming robots. That required the use of a portable cart of MacBooks, which could only be plugged in at the back of the room. This maneuver involved pushing two rows of desks out of the way. The desks weren't on wheels, so re-arranging them took some effort. And their surface tops were roughly the size of the closed boxes that held the Lego™ Robotics kits, so just opening them – let alone organizing and assembling pieces – required the combined surface tops of two desks. (I have helped sort and reorganize more than one Lego™ kit that fell on the floor.) Because the room was booked for other classes through the day, our equipment had to come and go with us. The pre-service teachers had only ten minutes between classes, which meant extra rushing to make it across campus for their inconveniently located next class. I was left on my own to get the MacBook cart out of the room and to reconfigure the desks to the arrangement posted on the wall.

In a nutshell, the space wasn't well suited to our needs. But the tasks demanded we adapt. We squeezed desks together. We tried to move the extra desks to the front of the room and double them up. Some groups went out to the halls and worked on the floors. I pushed my way to the back of the room, sometimes feeling stuck once I was there. While we never quite managed to configure the room in an ideal way, collaborative design conversations still emerged. Robots were built, programmed, and tested. New STEM learning tasks were prototyped and shared.

Consolidating Key Points

"What is learning?" Answer the question in three ways:

   List some synonyms. What words popped to mind right away when you heard the question?

   Compose a definition. How would you describe learning if you were required to write a dictionary entry?

   Draw a picture. What would you depict if you were asked for an image or icon to represent learning?

What is "learning"?

The question, "What is learning?" might seem an odd one to pose immediately after this opening narrative ... which might appear to be about the sorts of constraints and obstacles that teachers need to negotiate. That is, it probably seems to be more about things that frustrate learning than about learning itself.

But we see learning as the key issue in the narrative – or, more specifically, about implicit, enacted, uninterrogated beliefs about learning that channel decisions about formal education. For us, the key question isn't what the teacher might do to mitigate time constraints, space limitations, and so on (although these are certainly issues that, as recounted in the narrative, teachers must negotiate!). Rather, the burning issue is the belief system that gave rise to those constraints and limitations in the first place.

What must one believe about learning to structure classroom spaces in the manner described in the anecdote?

Answers to this question aren't simple. To offer a comprehensive response, we would have to reach back millennia into cultural obsessions on such matters as social order, metaphysics, and science. Definitions and interpretations of "learning" reside in hairballs of assumptions about identity, truth, understanding, teaching, and formal education. For that reason, learning is one of most troubling issues in the field of education.

For the most part, learning is a problematic issue for educators not because of what people are talking about, but because of what they're not talking about. Or, more precisely, when it comes to discussions of learning, it's usually not what's made explicit but what's left implicit that matters the most.

On that point, it might be tempting to think that the question, "What is learning?" has a definitive response. After all, everybody does it. We all know what it means to learn something. On top of that, learning has been the focus of intense scientific inquiry for a very long time. So, it only seems reasonable to expect that there would be comprehensive and more-or-less agreed-upon answers by now.

In this chapter's sidebars, we present some familiar artifacts of modern schooling as we invite you to consider the beliefs and theories of learning that might be invested in those artifacts.

That is, each artifact was informed by implicit assumptions – and, less often, explicit theories – about learning and learners. We invite you to critique and analyze these artifacts based on the learning theories presented in this chapter ... and to think about what more recent, evidence-based theories of learning might recommend.

Unfortunately, this isn't the case – and, for us, this point is especially evident in this chapter's opening anecdote. We read this episode as an instance of conflicting answers to the question, "What is learning?"

To explain, it has only been over the last few centuries that society has been making buildings that were principally designed and constructed as settings for learning. Formal education, as currently acted out in schools around the world, is barely a few centuries old. Prior to the emergence of the modern public school, education tended to occur in borrowed spaces – in churches, public squares, homes, and other locations that allowed people to gather. The forms and artifacts of the modern school, many of which are highlighted in this chapter's margin notes, are recent inventions for the most part, ones tethered to very specific beliefs about knowledge and learning.

Before delving into those beliefs, however, it will be helpful to be explicit about a few principles of human thinking that are supported by recent research in cognitive science – which, as mentioned in the previous chapter, is a transdisciplinary domain that brings together neuroscience, psychology, linguistics, education, and other disciplines around a shared interest in how humans learn. Two principles are especially relevant here:

- Human thinking is mostly analogical rather than logical.
- Ideas don't (and can't) exist in isolation.

The first of these points is a near contradiction to a deeply engrained assumption that humans are logical beings – that is, the belief that humans find it easy to move through linear arguments and to derive rational conclusions. In fact, people find logical deduction taxing and, frequently, unconvincing. In contrast, humans are adept at analogical thinking – that is, construing associations among diverse happenings, finding connections between very different sets of experiences, and mapping ideas from one domain onto another (Black, 1962; Lakoff & Johnson, 1999). The ease of such conceptual bridging not only differentiates human thinking from other creatures' thinking,

Think of what a typical classroom desk was designed to do:

- **keep bodies facing forward,**
- **separate individuals,**
- **fit easily into grid arrangements, and**
- **hold bodies still.**

Think of who this object was designed for – someone who ...

- **was right handed,**
- **was a specific height and size,**
- **had specific ranges of mobility.**

What would you have to believe about learning and learners to design a desk in this way?

it also distinguishes human capacities from machine capacities. The second point, that ideas do not exist is isolation, is just as important. Kelly (2010) phrased it more poetically:

> ideas never stand alone. They come woven in a web of auxiliary ideas, consequential notions, supporting concepts, foundational assumptions, side effects, and logical consequences and a cascade of subsequent possibilities. Ideas fly in flocks. To hold one idea in mind means to hold a cloud of them. (pp. 44–45)

We'll go into more detail in the next section on how these notions are useful for making sense of learning. For now it might be useful to think about some of the associations you bring to this complex phenomenon.

Consolidating Key Points

"Ideas never stand alone."

The vocabulary and images that are used to characterize learning aren't just *descriptions*. They're also *prescriptions*. That is, they have implications and consequences for how people act. For instance, if learning is construed as "acquiring" or "taking things in," it follows that teaching must be about "delivering" or "presenting" those things.

Look at the synonyms, definitions, and/or images that you assembled for the previous "Consolidating Key Points" (on p. 14). What sorts of synonyms, definitions, and images for "teaching" might fly in the same flock?

Learning theories

If you're a native speaker of English, there's a strong chance your answers to the "Consolidating Key Points" tasks, above, would include such notions as *acquiring, picking up, internalizing, taking in, getting,* or *grasping* – each of which is actually a metaphor. Moreover, each term is part of a popular flock of associations that collects around an assumption that knowledge is some sort of object that exists outside of learners, and that learning is a process of getting that knowledge-object from the outside to the inside.

That flock of associations, in fact, is behind some of the frustrations noted in this chapter's opening anecdote and that are so evident in modern schools, around such matters as productivity, efficiency, and parsimony. Or, more descriptively, it's part of an even grander flock of associations in which knowledge and learning are likened to manufactured and marketed objects. This cluster of analogies undergirds such modern educational emphases as standardization, evaluation, linearized curricula, and delivery-focused teaching methods. Awareness of this cluster of associations is useful for making sense of the lines and grids that are used to structure classroom spaces, lesson plans, school schedules, and many of the other rectilinear forms that are encountered in modern education.

So, is it reasonable to think about learning in terms of *getting a grasp on things* and its associated web of metaphors? This web is certainly a popular theory, perhaps even the dominant one. However, despite its prominence, this notion is a fiction. When learners learn, no *thing* moves from the outside to the inside; no *thing* is picked up; no *thing* is taken in.

Why should educators care? Metaphors are more than just figurative descriptions. They also carry prescriptions for practice. For example, as is developed in more detail below, the metaphor that *learning is acquisition* has influenced understandings of curriculum, especially around such matters as what is to be learned, how ideas are best formatted, and how people should teach. It is thus critical for curriculum developers, policy makers, teachers, and others involved in the educational process to be aware of how metaphors frame their beliefs about learning and how, in turn, those beliefs might shape the experiences of learners (Geary, 2011; Sfard, 1998).

Actualizing this suggestion is not as straightforward as it might at first seem. Metaphors are often invisible to users, as we might have inadvertently demonstrated in the previous chapter with our concern around why today's students are learning what they are learning. We have analyzed and re-analyzed our phrasing in that chapter, and it's taken a great deal of effort to get rid of terms associated with acquisition. We still

Think about some of the different classroom arrangements that you've experienced. Where is the learner located in each? How is the teacher positioned relative to learners? Who is doing what? Where are attentions focused, and what devices are used to focus that attention?

What principles of learning and learners are being enacted in the different settings?

haven't fully succeeded. But, to be fair to ourselves, removing all uses of this particular metaphor may be nearly impossible; it is the default mode for talking about learning among English-speakers.

In this chapter, we explore the suggestion that, while it is vital for STEM educators to ask questions about why students need to learn specific content, a prior question is "What is learning?" To address this matter, we present an overview of the diversity of theories that infuse and inform contemporary educational practices. We focus on elements that are useful for making critical discernments among the many theoretical offerings.

Perhaps the most sweeping change in classroom artifacts over the past few decades has been from blackboards to interactive whiteboards. In some instances, this shift prompted changes in teaching; in others, traditional practices persisted.

What are some of the different affordances of blackboards and whiteboards? What shifts in beliefs about learning might be needed to capitalize on different affordances?

Before diving in, it's important to be clear on what we mean by the word *theory*. So often heard as the opposite of *practice*, we see the two notions as inseparable. Every educational practice is associated with particular perspectives – that is, *theories* – on knowledge and learning. Simply stated, a theory is a way of seeing things, which is precisely what the word originally meant (from the Greek *theoria*, "a looking at, a viewing, a sight").

There are literally hundreds of theories of learning represented in the current educational literature. For example, one popular site (Learning-theories.com) catalogs more than 70 prominent perspectives, each classified as one of the following:

- Behaviorist Theories
- Cognitivist Theories
- Constructivist, Social, and Situational Theories
- Motivational and Humanist Theories
- Design Theories
- Descriptive and Meta Theories
- Identity Theories and Models
- Child Development Theories
- Media and Technology Theories
- Miscellaneous Theories.

Given their sheer numbers, it is clearly impractical to review all these perspectives. In fact, even the strategy of clustering them in the manner above can be problematic, in part, because these categories can amplify small differences while they obscure deep similarities.

To avoid these pitfalls, we focus less on categories

of theories and more on metaphors to highlight key conceptual commitments and to distinguish between "folk psychology" and empirically grounded scientific theories. Our starting place in this review of theories of learning is to look at everyday beliefs and common sense – that is, at the usually unquestioned webs of association that are evoked in everyday conversations, in popular culture, and in many classrooms.

Consolidating Key Points

Visit Learning-theories.com and click through the categories.

If you respond the way we did when we visited the site, you will probably feel a little daunted. Trying to understand learning theories by cataloguing them is overwhelming, and perhaps impossible. As many have noted, learning theories are like toothbrushes. Everyone has one, and no one wants to use anyone else's.

That's why we don't catalogue theories in this book. Rather, we look at their underlying metaphors and their flocks of association. It turns out that there are only a few such flocks flying around at the moment, and so this approach can afford surprising power in discussions of the nature of learning.

Folk theories: *Learning is acquiring, discovering, journeying, or constructing*

Over the past several centuries, some of the metaphors that have been developed to characterize learning have included loading a catapult, writing on a slate, setting a printing press, taking a photograph, wiring a switchboard, filming a movie, and programming a computer. Based on our own surveys of these and other images, our impression is that there are four especially popular clusters:

- Cluster 1: knowledge as object, learners as containers, learning as filling the container with acquired objects;
- Cluster 2: knowledge as hidden treasure, learners as seekers, learning as discovering;
- Cluster 3: knowledge as territories, learners as travelers, learning as progressing; and
- Cluster 4: knowledge as constructions, learners as builders, learning as putting things together.

At first glance, these clusters of association might seem conceptually distinct from one another. But there are some important commonalities. For instance, across all of them, knowledge is presented as something stable, pre-existing, and separate from knowers; learners are cast as deficient beings that are isolated from one another and insulated from the world. And learning is all about overcoming deficiencies.

Collectively, these folk beliefs on knowledge and learning have underpinned and infused schooling practices for centuries. Each is part of a grander web of associations that includes descriptions of and advice on matters of curriculum and pedagogy (Schubert, 1986). Tables 2.1, 2.2, 2.3, and 2.4 (on the next two pages) point at some aspects of these webs.

As is developed later, the main issue here is not whether any of these clusters of association is "correct," since it's unlikely that the phenomenon of learning will ever be adequately represented by any single perspective. The task of characterizing learning in all its incredible complexity continues to require multiple theories and diverse images – and so the principal concern is not rightness-vs.-wrongness, but usefulness (Bransford, Brown, & Cocking, 1999; Schubert, 1986). How does each cluster orient attentions and actions? How does it enable or constrain the efforts of educators?

The metaphors presented in the tables on the next pages have been broadly criticized for being more constraining than enabling. The following criticisms have been particularly prominent around the way these notions have played out in formal education:

- Knowledge tends to be seen as fixed facts to be memorized and standardized procedures to be mastered.
- Learners tend to be assumed / projected as radically separated individuals who are insulated from the world and isolated from one another.
- Education tends to be presented as a project of delivery, whereby learners are positioned more as passive recipients than active agents.
- Learning tends to be cast as a linear, standardized process – a notion that relies on the associated assumption that there is such a thing as a "normal learner." (Dumont, Istance, & Benavides, 2010)

This image could be depicting almost any high school hallway in North America – a straight corridor with equally spaced classrooms that are likely separated by age/grade level and subject area.

Where else are straight lines and linear trajectories – used both literally (e.g., to structure buildings) and metaphorically (e.g., to plan lessons) – evident in traditional schooling? How are such lines reflective of and supported by beliefs about learning and learners?

Table 2.1: Popular associations and implications of "learning as acquisition"

Phenomenon	Metaphors	Assumptions/Entailments	Sample Usages
Knowledge	Object; commodity	Knowledge is stable; it exists independently of knowers.	"The truth is out there." "Cold hard facts."
Learning	Acquiring; internalizing	Learning is moving knowledge from the outside to the inside.	"Grasping the point." "Taking things in." "Getting it." "Picking things up." "Cramming for a test."
Learner	Container	Learners are deficient. They need to be filled or completed.	"Great capacity for learning." "I can hold a lot in my head." "He's a sponge."
Education	Decomposed knowledge	Reducing knowledge to bite-sized bits makes it more ingestable/internalizable.	"There's too much stuff in the curriculum." "Regurgitate the material for the exam."

Table 2.2: Popular associations and implications of "learning as discovering"

Phenomenon	Metaphors	Assumptions/Entailments	Sample Usages
Knowledge	Hidden object	Objects are either concealed (in darkness) or apparent (illuminated). If apparent, they are aspects of knowledge.	"Shine some light on the subject." "Hide the truth by keeping them in the dark."
Learning	Discovering	Learning is about uncovering, revealing, or "shining a light" on previously "unseen" parts of the world.	"See what I'm saying?" "Suddenly the lights went on." "Enlighten me."
Learner	Seeker	Humans enter the world knowledge-blind and gradually see more and more.	"He's still in the dark." "Is that clear?" "Seek the truth."
Education	Processes to enable insight, enlightenment.	Structuring experiences with a view toward increased clarity and abilities to see more.	"Show them the way." "Path to enlightenment." "Hoping for a brighter future."

Table 2.3: Popular associations and implications of "learning as journeying"

Phenomenon	Metaphors	Assumptions/Entailments	Sample Usages
Knowledge	Territory; field	Knowledge exists in tidy, discrete regions.	"The field of geography." "What's your area?"
Learning	Journeying; progressing	Learning is about becoming familiar with a field /area.	"We're getting there." "There's a short cut." "We're stuck on a step." "Going in circles."
Learner	Traveler; explorer	Learners move through domains of knowledge.	"Discovery learning." "Quick learner."
Education	Pathway	Learning can be made efficient by tracing out a direct route through a field.	"Learning trajectories." "Follow the curriculum." "Where are you in math?" "Advanced studies." "We need to backtrack." "Accelerated programs."

Table 2.4: Popular associations and implications of "learning as assembling"

Phenomenon	Metaphors	Assumptions/Entailments	Sample Usages
Knowledge	Edifice	Knowledge systems begin with premises, from which more complex assertions are derived ... and so on.	"Build on the facts." "That argument doesn't hold together."
Learning	Assembling	Learning is assembling bits of insight into more sophisticated understandings.	"Put it together." "Everyone constructs their own understandings."
Learner	Builder	Completed knowledge can't be transferred; rather, each person must re-assemble it from the bits provided.	"She has a solid knowledge of physics." "Her knowledge of history is shaky."
Education	Tower	Curriculum should start with basics/foundations and proceed upward.	"We'll build on this next year." "Which level are you on?"

Importantly, a great deal of research into learning has been oriented by these assumptions. (See, e.g., Carey, 2014, for a popular review.) Indeed, as has been demonstrated across centuries of standardized educational practice, it is quite possible to structure entire schooling systems around such convictions. To illustrate this point, consider the first term in each of the dyads we use to frame the STEM domains:

Science ((**method**) inquiring)
Technology ((**usage**) designing)
Engineering ((**application**) innovating)
Mathematics ((**calculation**) modeling).

We sum these up with two overarching notions:

Learning ((**acquisition**) participating)
STEM Education ((**recipient**) contributing).

Do a bit of research to learn about the origins of grid-based schedules made up of 45-minute lesson blocks. What were designers focused on? What might they have been thinking, vis-à-vis learning?

In other words, curricular emphases on method, use, application, calculation – that is, on getting and employing finished ideas – are all evidence of a prevailing assumption that learners are receptacles or recipients.

For us, that's a curious situation, as we are aware of *no empirical evidence whatsoever that shows that the metaphor of "learning as acquiring" is a valid description* of what goes on when people learn. We thus turn to theories that have been subjected to more rigorous examination, both conceptually and empirically. We invite you to consider how the second terms in the above dyads are foregrounded as necessary aspects of education within these theories.

Think back to your own experience of being deeply immersed in learning (not necessarily in school). How did you experience time? How might an imposed time limit have affected your engagement?

Consolidating Key Points

"Brain as computer" is the metaphor that underpins a theory of learning known as "cognitivism" – which is one of the most popular folk theories of learning at the moment.

Among its flock of associated metaphors are such notions as "knowledge as information," "perception as inputting data," and "thinking as processing."

How is the learner seen in this frame? How is education cast? What are some of the analogical entailments for teaching? Assemble a table (similar to those on the previous pages) of this popular web of metaphors.

Behaviorist theories: *Learning is linking stimulus and response, leading to observable changes in behavior.*

The early-20th century saw a dramatic shift in thinking about human cognition as researchers, principally in psychology, began to problematize commonsensical interpretations of learning and to seek more robust models that could be supported with empirical evidence. Several theories were proposed, but behaviorism dominated through the first half of the century – in part because it aligned itself with the "hard sciences" by focusing exclusively on observable and measurable phenomena.

As with every cluster of theories, there is much variation among the perspectives gathered under this header. The first behaviorisms were based mainly on experiments with animals and their cause–effect conclusions were extrapolated to humans. Much later, more "radical" behaviorisms incorporated distinctly human qualities, such as how emotion figures into conceptual understanding, the social dimensions of motivation, and so on.

These buildings have very similar architectures ... but very different functions. The one above is a school, and the one below is a jail.

Through the 1700s and 1800s, the same set of principles was used for designing both prisons and schools. Based on these images, what were some of these principles? What similarities between learners and felons might have been assumed?

However, there are a few elements that are common to all behaviorisms. Firstly, behaviorists rejected the belief that knowledge is some sort of external, stable, and context-free object that exists independently of knowers. They explicitly redefined personal knowledge as established and stable repertoires of behavior that are triggered by events in the world (Skinner, 1950). Secondly, behaviorists insisted on observable and measureable data, and this insistence was reflected in a definition of learning as changes in behavior that are due to environmental circumstances (Thorndike, 1931).

This movement revolves around the metaphor that *learning is linking triggers and reactions.* For behaviorists, the process of creating links between environmental stimuli and the individual's responses was seen as predictable and mechanical – manageable through well-timed rewards and punishments. Key elements in this cluster of metaphors are summarized in Table 2.5, on the next page.

By the middle of the 20th century, behaviorisms were the dominant theories of learning within education,

Table 2.5: Associations and implications of behaviorist theories of learning

Phenomenon	Metaphors
Knowing	Behaviorial repertoire; the range of responses triggered by stimuli in the knower's environment
Learning	Changes in behavior (linking stimuli to responses)
Learner	Reactor (to stimuli)
Education	Carefully engineered and highly repetitive sequence of conditioning experiences governed by feedback regimes

and their influence is still evident in requirements for measurable learning outcomes, linear lesson plans, and well-defined schemes for rewards and punishments. Over recent decades, however, these theories have been largely rejected by educators, mostly because of the emphasis on control. For example, implementing a truly behaviorist curriculum would require that every aspect of the learner's environment be carefully managed to an extent that is simply not tenable in real classrooms. As well, such a curriculum would not just ignore human creativity but actively suppress it, as the educator attempts to govern the (observable) connections that learners make. Some of these issues can be seen in relationship to inherited assumptions that were carried forward from commonsensical folk theories of learning. These convictions include that learning happens entirely inside the head, the learner is hermetically sealed, the child is deficient, and education is a mechanical cause–effect process that is imposed onto a largely passive student.

On the more positive side, behaviorisms contributed to some important shifts in thinking. For example, they helped to expose the inadequacies of folk psychology, they reminded educators of the importance of context, they amplified the role of motivation in learning, they shifted educators' attention from assumed-to-be-stable *knowledge* to dynamic-and-shifting *knowing*, and the new metaphor of *learning as making links* exposed untenable assumptions about *acquiring* and *taking in objects*. Thus, even though many contemporary learning theories reject some of the core tenets of behaviorism, they share and elaborate some key insights.

This image is from the Alberta Mathematics Program of Study (Alberta Education, 2014). Like most guides, it presents subject matter as a sequence of parsed bits of knowledge or organized into a grid.

John Franklin Bobbitt and Ralph Tyler were two prominent advocates of this relatively recent model of curriculum. Both focused on efficiency as a principle of educational design. Do some research on them. What might they have believed about learning and learners, more generally, to have advocated this model of curriculum?

Consolidating Key Points

Click on the "Behaviorism" button on the Learning-theories.com website and browse some of the information presented. Names that should be (or should become) familiar to educators include Pavlov, Thorndike, and Skinner.

Although behaviorisms have been subject to intense criticism since the mid-20th century, many principles persist. A likely reason for the ongoing influence is that many assumptions blend well with popular folk beliefs. Compare Table 2.5 with Tables 2.1–2.4 (and your new table, if you did the previous "Consolidating Key Points" exercise). How are the theories compatible? Where do they diverge?

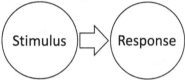

Nowhere is the implicit linearity of modern schooling more evident than in standardized templates for lesson planning.

Do searches for "lesson plan" and "lesson plan templates." How do these artifacts compel users to think about teaching? What affordances do standardized templates provide for diversities among learners? What affordances do they provide for situation-focused, constructionist theories of learning? How might you design a template to accommodate different learners and different situations?

Constructivist theories: *Learning is construing sense*

Although behaviorisms dominated discussions of learning through much of the 20th century, they represent only a narrow slice of research-informed theories to emerge over the last 100 years. Another important strand that arose in parallel were constructivist theories that focus on individual sense-making.

This cluster of theories has been subject to widespread misinterpretation because it might appear that their core metaphor is *learning is constructing*. That's actually incorrect, and the problem traces back to a mistranslation that has persisted for many decades. The word *constructivism* was borrowed from French, where its verb root of *construire* can be translated as either "to construe" or "to construct." It is now evident that most of the authors of these theories, particularly Piaget (1954), intended the former meaning. That is, these theories assert that learners construe their own understandings – indeed, that humans are compelled to impose structure on the world. Learning is an ongoing process of sense-making; it is not a matter of building internal edifices of objective knowledge but construing and imposing webs of subjective sense.

The metaphors at the core of these theories – i.e., that *knowing is an evolving ecosystem of associations* and that *learning is an adaptive dynamic of making sense* – bear a resemblance to the metaphors of behaviorisms. Both clusters of theories focus on connections and associations. What is significantly different, however, is how the dynamics of learning are described. Behaviorisms, like most folk theories, align with physics and the cause–effect dynamics of Newtonian mechanics. In contrast, constructivisms align more with biology, describing learning in terms of the organic, developmental imagery of Darwinian evolution. In the process, constructivisms problematize assumptions about the controllability of learning.

With regard to education, the implications of these shifts in metaphor and emphasis are immense. For example, within this frame the longstanding curricular tradition of focusing on facts and skills is seen as naïve, since human learning is more about meaning-making than mechanical reproduction. The notion of a one-size-fits-all, standardized curriculum is similarly criticized, since learners can never construe the same meanings as one another. The reason is straightforward: the raw materials of knowing are one's experiences in the world. Each learner has a distinct set of experiences, and so each learner's web of associations must be unique. The best that can be hoped for, then, is compatible (but never identical) interpretations among learners. Table 2.6 summarizes some key aspects of the metaphors at the heart of constructivist theories.

Advice for educators from constructivist theorists tends to focus on experiences that support compatible interpretations. Suggestions include orienting attentions to specific aspects of phenomena, encouraging similar actions for learners, inviting shared inquiry in which learners announce and rehearse meanings, and taking care in selecting tools of interpretation (e.g., vocabulary and theories). Importantly, these aspects

Age	USA Canada Australia India	UK	Korea	Japan
3	EC1	Nursery	Playhouse	
4	EC2	Reception	K	
5	K	Year 1	K	
6	Grade 1	Year 2	Grade 1	Grade 1
7	Grade 2	Year 3	Grade 2	Grade 2
8	Grade 3	Year 4	Grade 3	Grade 3
9	Grade 4	Year 5	Grade 4	Grade 4
10	Grade 5	Year 6	Grade 5	Grade 5
11	Grade 6	Year 7	Grade 6	Grade 6
12	Grade 7	Year 8	Grade 7	Grade 7
13	Grade 8	Year 9	Grade 8	Grade 8
14	Grade 9	Year 10	Grade 9	Grade 9
15	Grade 10	Year 11	Grade 10	Grade 10
16	Grade 11	Year 12	Grade 11	Grade 11
17	Grade 12	Year 13	Grade 12	Grade 12

An almost universal schooling practice is to sort learners based only on their birthdates. This practice traces back centuries and is rooted in folk theories.

Constructivisms offered a different strategy for clustering learners, based on developmental levels. Do some research on developmentalisms. How might they challenge age-indexed grade levels? Which current practices might they bolster?

Table 2.6: Associations and implications of constructivist theories of learning

Phenomenon	Metaphors
Knowing	Personal coherence; one's evolving ecosystem of associations
Learning	Ongoing adaptive dynamic of construing personal coherence
Learner	Sufficient, active agent
Education	Structured engagements that are designed to orient attentions, demand action, invite inquiry, and encourage particular families of associations

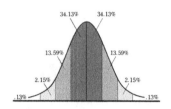

The "normal distribution" was originally developed to understand patterns across games of chance and insurable phenomena. It was imported into education in the late 1800s on the assumption that differences among humans were similarly distributed. It continues to be used to sort children according to their performance and (dis)abilities.

What must one think about learning to sort and cluster students in this manner? Which learning theories support this mode of classification?

of "inquiry learning" are a far cry from the "discovery learning" approach, which is in fact anchored to folk understandings of learning. Unlike the unsupported web of assumptions that are used to describe discovery learning approaches, inquiry learning is highly structured, requires a teacher with considerable disciplinary expertise, and does not abandon children to derive their own conclusions. While it does not succumb to the fallacy that learning can be *determined by* curricula and teaching, it strongly aligns with the conviction that learning is *dependent on* curricula and teaching.

Such implications are tethered to the assumption that learners are sufficient rather than deficient beings. That is, each learner occupies a coherent world. The point of education, then, is not to fill a void but to present challenges that prompt learners to reconfigure or elaborate their worlds. In other words, education in this frame isn't something that is done to a learner, but a process that engages a learner. Departing radically from folk theories, learners are regarded as integrated, active agents. Moreover, humans are recognized to be compulsive sense-makers, unable to suppress the tendency to make sense of experiences ... but, unfortunately, prone to clinging to subjectively satisfying beliefs, even in the face of objectively verified facts.

Consolidating Key Points

Compare the contents of Table 2.4 and Table 2.6. The flock of metaphors presented in Table 2.4 is sometimes called "trivial constructivism," and the flock in Table 2.6 is sometimes called "radical constructivism." How are they similar? Different?

(Regarding these questions, a critical distinction between folk theories and constructivist theories is that the former tend to frame learning in terms of "steady accumulation," whereas the latter frames learning in terms of "recursive elaboration." Look into the meanings of these phrases. How do they position learners?)

Many educational theorists and researchers assert that these clusters have virtually nothing in common and attending to more radical notions will lead to very different sorts of teaching. Do the contrasts you noted between the contents of Tables 2.4 and 2.6 prompt you to think in that direction?

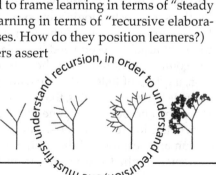

Socio-cultural theories: *Learning is participation*

In the latter half of the 20th century, there was a dramatic shift toward transdisciplinarity in discussions of learning. Up to that point, learning was mainly treated as an issue in psychology. In fact, up to about the 1970s, education was commonly defined as an "applied psychology." But, at about that time, researchers in education began to demonstrate that learning also had sociological and anthropological dimensions.

A major trigger in this shift was an emergent awareness of the collective aspects of learning. For example, researchers in sociology began to emphasize the role of social groups on the development of understanding (Berger & Luckmann, 1967). The resulting cluster of theories is known collectively as "constructionisms," which includes social constructivism, sociocultural theory, activity theory, actor-network theory, critical theory, and many other specific perspectives. Although these theories are by no means identical, they have important commonalities. For example, they view knowledge as inseparable from action. In other words, "knowledge" is everything entailed by participation within a cultural milieu (e.g., language, symbols, tools, shared meaning).

Most important to this cluster of theories is the assertion that learning occurs within social interaction. Situation-focused constructionisms embrace the constructivist assertion that each learner's construals are necessarily unique. However, they add that sense-making is a situated, dialogical process, not an isolated, monological one. In other words, individuals actively make sense of their environment through cooperative interaction, using the same vocabularies, surrounded by the same technologies, exposed to similar challenges, and so on. Stated more provocatively, while the individual is recognized as a "learning system," the communities in which the learner is embedded (e.g., a group of fellow students) are also regarded as systems that learn – that is, that seek coherence, impose structure, and otherwise generate knowledge.

Scholars interested in the social and cultural aspects of human learning and the nested nature of learning systems sought to draw attention to the manners

There's a good chance you've written a test in an examination hall similar to the one in the above image. Notice its similarities to the factory-model depicted in the image below. The similarity isn't accidental. Seeking efficiency, order, and ease of surveillance, schools adopted the mode of organization more than a century ago.

What must one think about learning to organize classrooms around principles of efficiency, order, and ease of monitoring?

Most constructivist and constructionist theories explicitly reject these principles. What alternatives might they offer?

in which situations – that is, languages, roles, technologies, social classes, and other aspects of context – figured into knowing and learning. Arguments and evidence arose that made it apparent that knowing and learning do not simply happen inside individuals. Rather, these phenomena are distributed across and integrated with all aspects of knowers' situations. That set the stage for a new, challengingly different metaphor: *learning is participation* (Lave & Wenger, 1991).

In this frame, knowing and knowledge are interpreted as situated action in a grander system – that is, the sorts of behaviors, engagements, and interpretations that are appropriate in, called forth by, enabled within, and constrained by a situation. In this sense, knowing and learning are "doubly embodied" (Merleau-Ponty, 1962). They involve collective bodies / learners (e.g., student bodies; the body politic) that unfold from and are enfolded in biological bodies / learners. In other words; knowing, doing, and being are inseparable. That is, these theories assert that questions of learning cannot be considered independent of questions of identity and context. In Table 2.7, we summarize some of the key metaphors in this cluster of theories, along with a suggestion as to how curriculum might be conceived within this frame.

This way of looking at the reflexive relationship between one's knowing and one's being is much more than the assertion that learning is a combination of nature and nurture. It is, more accurately, that biology and situation are so intertwined that it makes little sense to consider them as separate elements. Rather than thinking in terms of separable influences, they

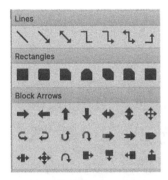

Lines, rectangles, and arrows are pervasive in modern schooling – so pervasive that it can be very difficult to think about other possible forms for informing and organizing schooling.

Evidence for this assertion is presented in almost every margin image in this chapter.

Can you think of alternatives?

Table 2.7: Associations and implications of constructionist theories of learning

Phenomenon	Metaphors
Knowing	Situated action (called forth by and enabled through collectivity)
Learning	Participating; becoming
Learner	Situated agent, embodying and embodied by the collective ... or, more broadly, any complex adaptive form, ranging from the subcellular to the planetary
Education	Engagements that promote awareness of social, cultural, and ecological situatedness while supporting ethical action

are better cast as nested phenomena – biological bodies within social bodies within cultural bodies – with
influences flowing both inward and outward.

Some learning theorists have pressed the discussion
even further, in both micro and macro directions. We
attempt to illustrate this point in Figure 2.1, in which
different academic domains and learning theories are
linked to learning (eco)systems that span the subper-
sonal through the planetary.

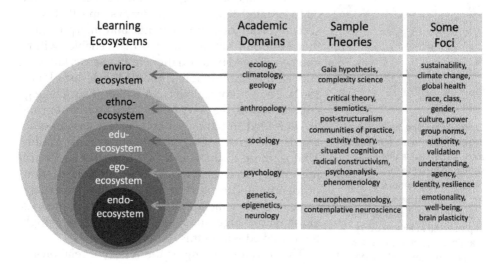

Figure 2.1: A visual metaphor for interpreting relationships among contemporary theories
of learning (Davis, Sumara, & Luce-Kapler, 2015; used with permission)

Importantly, this sensibility is not entirely new. In
many pre-modern, Indigeneous, and/or nonwestern
cultures, learning is characterized as a systemic totality
that comprises minds, bodies, communities, cultures,
and the more-than-human world. (See, e.g., https://
firstnationspedagogy.com/CCL_Learning_Model_FN.pdf;
https://firstnationspedagogy.com/CCL_Inuit_Holistic_
Learning_Model_EN.pdf; https://firstnationspedagogy.com/
CCL_Learning_Model_MET.pdf.) Emerging theories
might thus be better described as recoveries of long-
forgotten insights than as major developments in
thinking.

Consolidating Key Points

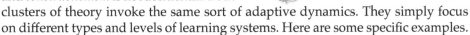

The similarity of the words *constructivism* and *constructionism* is not accidental. Both clusters of theory invoke the same sort of adaptive dynamics. They simply focus on different types and levels of learning systems. Here are some specific examples.

- Jean Piaget and Bärbel Inhelder focused on the individual's construal of a coherent web of associations and interpretations.

- Jerome Bruner focused on perceptions and sensation, seeing them as active rather than passive processes.

- Lev Vygotsky saw personal learning as embedded in and emerging through social connections and actions in a cultural environment.

- Seymour Papert's research into learning revolved around developing and examining technological interfaces between children and dynamic artifacts.

Piaget, Inhelder, and Bruner are often cited as among the principal authors of constructivism – that is, theories of learning that focus on the individual. Vygotsky and Papert are among the most highly regarded constructionists, as they extended their interests in learning to include the material world, technologies, social relations, and cultural context.

On the Learning-theories.com website, constructivist and constructionist theories are collapsed into the same category, namely "Constructivist, Social and Situated Theories." Click on the entries under that header and discuss whether each of the theories presented is better characterized as constructivist or constructionist.

Summing up

The field of education has always been rife with tensions and conflicts. For example, the common debate over whether schooling should serve the needs of the individual or the needs of society was a popular topic among the ancient Greeks, as was the tension between objective truth and subjective interpretation.

Incompatible learning theories are a major source of such tensions. Paradoxically, however, most theories were initially developed and positioned as ways to overcome these sorts of tensions by alerting educators of underlying assumptions and indefensible beliefs.

It's important to be aware that the STEM domains haven't been silent here. On the contrary, each has contributed greatly to both theoretical frames and empirical evidence. Currently, with regard to the theories discussed in this chapter, the weight of evidence suggests that folk theories and behaviorist theories are inadequate for informing teaching practice, and that constructivist and socio-cultural theories are reasonably defensible interpretations of the complex processes associated with different aspects of learning.

In this regard, we encourage you to look into the transdisciplinary domain of cognitive science, mentioned earlier. Often defined as the "scientific study of the mind," cognitive science is an evidence-driven domain that has provided important and useful insights into strategies and structures that might support learning (see, e.g., Willingham, 2009) ...

... but it is all but silent on matters of what should be learned and why it's good to know. For help on those matters, we turn to the disciplines themselves in the next chapters.

Learning Challenges

1. Pretend you were just asked to help a second-language learner understand the word *learning*. How would you describe it? What would you link it to? What sorts of examples would you use?

    After you've recorded your responses to these questions, try to pick out the metaphors you've used. Compare those metaphors to the analyses presented in Tables 2.1 to 2.7. Do your metaphors align with any of the clusters? Are you using multiple metaphors? If so, are they compatible?

    Consider your answers to these questions in relation to your responses to the "Consolidating Key Points" exercises at the start of the chapter. Has your thinking changed at all? How do your descriptions and examples of learning mesh with the various theories of learning discussed in the chapter?

2. Think back to a powerful learning experience that you've had, either inside or outside of school. What were you learning? Why were you learning it? How were you learning it? Where were you, and does that matter? Which learning theories help you make sense of why the learning experience was powerful for you? Are the clusters of metaphors presented in Tables 2.6 and 2.7 useful for answering these questions?

3. Assuming that you're involved as either a teacher or a student right now, think about your current experiences in formal education. Can you identify principles or theories of learning that are orienting the teacher's actions? Are they consistent? Are they defensible? Are they effective? If you have any advice to inform the situation, how would you frame it?

Chapter 3

Mathematics

calculation   modeling

IN BRIEF

Education has long equated "math" with symbol-based calculation, but it might be better understood in terms of modeling – that is, of developing tools to interpret the world.

The associative nature of **learning** is emphasized. We highlight how mathematical understandings arise as learners encounter and integrate diverse instantiations of concepts.

Teaching math has traditionally been cast as a logical sequential process, but it might be more appropriate to place more emphasis on experience, activity, imagery, and analogy.

Modeling Challenges   VIDEO LINK: https://vimeo.com/135695728

Trigonometric functions are part of the pre-calculus course at the Grade-12 level in Alberta Education's (2008) Program of Studies. The guide indicates that students "should be able to perform, analyze, and describe transformations on sinusoidal functions" (p. 52). There are several things to notice about the way that this curriculum outcome is stated:

- The competencies are all abstract – that is, they involve manipulation of symbols and the recall of definitions.
- There's no indication that "sinusoidal functions" can and should be a meaningful part of each learner's world;
- It might feel like "sinusoidal functions" is a hermetically sealed topic; there is little indication of its connections to other ideas in the network of mathematics.

Summing up: there is little room for mathematical meaning – that is, for bringing mathematics to life and for bringing it into one's life – in the way the curriculum outcome is stated.

Aware of that detail, Kathy resolved to structure her unit differently. Rather than focusing exclusively on abstract symbolic manipulations, she incorporated opportunities to study phenomena that can be modeled using the smooth undulations of the familiar sine curve. As Kathy noted at the start of the video, the unit began with explicit lessons on some features of sinusoidal functions, such as phase shift, period, and amplitude. These concepts were chosen because she knew they would be useful for the modeling tasks.

Students were assigned randomly to one of ten unique lab stations. Each station was centered on a phenomenon that was intended to highlight a key element of periodic sinusoidal functions. Students were tasked with mathematically modeling what they observed – that is, with creating a representation of the problem, figuring out what data they needed to gather, collecting those data, visually representing those data, completing a formal lab report, and ultimately generating an equation to model their observations.

As students worked independently in the classroom, Kathy circulated among the groups and stations to answer questions, formatively assess understandings, pose appropriate queries, and provide feedback. Her engagements with students were strategic: she aimed to scaffold student understanding through, for example, helping with appropriate usage of mathematical terminology as they articulated problems, described observations, and explicated solutions.

The approach wasn't lost on students. Instead of the frequently heard complaint, "When are we going to use this?", it was clear that class participants were aware that the mathematics they were studying was about their worlds. One student explained how he initially struggled with understanding trigonometry. He appreciated being able to take "the info that we found and turn it into a graph, to actually see it and be able to make your own graph rather than having one given to you, so you're able see how the values affect the graph." For him, "It helped a lot." Another student was excited about how trigonometric functions are found in the world. Her experience with the tasks helped her recognize how these concepts might actually be relevant in her everyday life, "which is cool … it just deepens the understanding. It makes you want to be part of the learning process."

After groups of students had adequate time to grapple with their labs, they were invited to compare their observations and equations with the products of other groups working with other phenomena. It didn't take long for them to realize that the phenomena at the different stations all had periodic cycles as well as maximum and minimum values. (These concepts are explored in the sidebars in this chapter.) Occurrences as diverse as spinning Ferris wheels, bouncing springs, rotating bicycle wheels, and swinging metronomes could all be represented with sinusoidal functions. That is, in this class, the mathematics was mainly about *modeling*, not *calculating*.

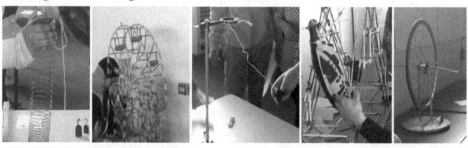

Consolidating Key Points

Use Google Image to do searches of "basic math," "basics," "school math," "math," and similar terms. What do you notice? What conceptions of "mathematics" might these images be projecting? Do those conceptions lean more toward calculating (i.e., about using memorized facts, performing symbolic operations, getting right answers, etc.) or more toward modeling (i.e., interpreting real-life situations, describing experiences in mathematical terms)?

Do your observations and interpretations resonate with your beliefs about school mathematics? If so, can you be more explicit about those beliefs? If not, what sorts of images might be more reflective of your understandings of mathematics?

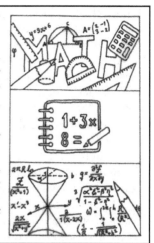

STE**M** Education

Our guess is that many – and maybe most – observers of Kathy's class wouldn't recognize much of what was going on as "doing math." After all, few of the markers of mathematics class were present. There were no textbooks, there were no practice exercises, there were no quizzes, and the focus wasn't calculation.

That the activity might not be seen as especially mathematical isn't surprising, given the deep history and pervasive presence of a calculation-focused version of school math. On that count, if you were to examine the earliest mathematics textbooks in English (e.g., Recorde, 1540), you'd notice some strong similarities to their modern counterparts. In particular, much of the content is the same, with the bulk of the emphases on arithmetic and algebra. But the similarities don't end there. The examples, explanations, and exercises provided in ancient textbooks are often very similar to the ones encountered today, especially when it comes to questions involving money and measurement.

The foci of school math have not only been remarkably stable across recent centuries, they are also strikingly consistent across jurisdictions. If you were to compare the mathematics curriculum in your home region to almost any other place in the developed world, you'd likely find almost identical lists of

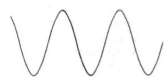

The images in this chapter's margins represent some familiar instantiations of trigonometric functions – specifically, phenomena (1) that can be modeled using the sine function and (2) that may thus be useful for developing a rich set of examples to support understandings. These examples are classified using Bruner's (1966) distinctions among of *enactive*, *iconic*, and *symbolic* representations.

topics, clustered and sequenced in very similar ways, and monitored with examinations that differ little from one country to the next.

And so you might be forgiven for drawing the conclusion that school mathematics is stable and universal. But, in fact, school mathematics has been the site of some of the most heated arguments on how people learn, what they should study, and how they should be taught. In North America, debates of these topics have been dubbed the "Math Wars," a phrase that hints at the intensity of squabbles that erupted about 50 years ago and that have persisted ever since (DeMott, 1962).

At the risk of oversimplifying, the Math Wars revolve around a distinction between a "traditional" focus on procedural competence (mainly in arithmetic and algebra) and different "reform" agendas that have been concerned with conceptual understanding. As the argument goes, the traditional math curriculum was designed to meet the basic numeracy needs of a society in the early stages of industrialization. Hence its emphases on calculation, measurement, nomenclature, and other rote competencies. Such knowledge was vital in an era when rapid industrialization met with limited numeracy skills.

Notice the shape of the profiles of spiral staircases and cork-screws. These forms can serve as *enactive* representations of sinusoidal functions – that is, instantiations that can be physically experienced.

What other physical forms with sine-like curves have you encountered?

But is what was "basic" then still basic now? Many argue that it isn't, including young learners who rightly question, "When am I going to use this?" In response, since the mid-1900s, several reforms have been attempted – and, as will be discussed in this chapter, the efforts continue. Such are the issues that frame this chapter: What mathematics is important to know in this day and age? How should it be known? What sorts of schooling experiences might support that knowing?

As far as the Math Wars go, we've elected not to pay much attention to that matter. Our reason is simple: it doesn't make much sense to us to think about "procedural competence" and "conceptual understanding" as a dichotomy – that is, two distinct, competing phenomena. On the contrary, we see these as co-entangled, necessarily complementary parts of the same whole. Attempting to develop one without nurturing the other will almost certainly compromise both.

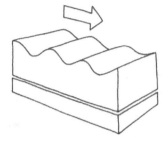

Some enactive instantiations are dynamic, involving the body in ways that static forms cannot. One example in this category is the wave pattern created by water ripples. A cross section can be modeled with a sine curve ... and the periodicity of the curve can be directly experienced by sitting in a boat that rises and falls with the waves.

Instead of focusing on that problematic dyad, this chapter is developed around a critical examination of the evolution of mathematics and its role in society. When first instituted as a core subject in newly formed public schools of the early Industrial Revolution, the explicit intention of school mathematics was to ensure that all future workers had basic skills in arithmetic, with lesser emphases on introductory competencies in algebra and geometry. The most important qualities of this knowing were speed and accuracy, as there were no other means to do necessary calculations and errors could be costly. Rote competence that was unburdened by the intricacies of conceptual understanding made sense at the time. The skills offered were truly "basic" to existence – that is, vital for and necessary to everyday life in a newly industrialized, urbanized, and consumerist setting.

If anything, such needs have increased in our current number- and data-dense worlds. However, knowing *how* to compute is no longer sufficient; it's just as important to know *when* and *why* to invoke different mathematical ideas. Phrased differently, "doing math" in today's world is about much more than *calculating*. Being mathematically competent is also about *modeling* – that is, being able to interpret and simulate real-life situations with mathematical constructs.

To our observation, Kathy's trigonometry unit was all about modeling, which is not to say they weren't calculating. In fact, their lab reports involved many more calculations than typical textbook exercises. But the students were gaining insight into much more than calculating the missing sides and angles of triangles. They were learning how to see trigonometric relationships in their worlds, and that sort of seeing is the essence of modeling.

Consolidating Key Points

Do a Google Image search for "math icon." What sorts of images come up? If you were asked to select one as an icon for your own teaching, which would you pick? (Or, what would you design?) Why?

What is "mathematics education"?

The history of school mathematics is, in many ways, a history of formal education in the western world. Although a modern school curriculum might seem unified and coherent, in fact it is better viewed as a blend of many different philosophies and beliefs on knowledge, learning, and teaching. For instance, a critical debate on the nature of mathematics is lurking inside almost every curriculum document and every classroom textbook. Is mathematics discovered or created? That is, is it inscribed in the universe, objectively true, independent of humans, and eternal – in which case it should be taught directly and tested objectively? Or is it an ever-evolving product of human ingenuity – in which case, modes of inquiry and argumentation should be highlighted?

We don't aim to resolve such disputes here. Rather, we focus on matters of productive and empowering ways of thinking about school mathematics. To that end, it is helpful to highlight some critical details in the history of mathematics.

For starters, the word *mathematics* referred to something very different when it was first coined. Its original meaning was something along the lines of "important learnings," derived from the Greek *mathema*, "that which is learned" (*O.E.D.*, Weiner et al., 1993). It was thus used to describe many topic areas, some of which would be readily recognized as mathematical today (e.g., arithmetic, geometry, and logic), and others less so (e.g., astronomy and music).

Usage of *mathematic* persisted until the 1600s, when the plural form *mathematics* suddenly sprang into popular usage. Until that moment in history, the word mathematics would have been heard as a collection of topics, not a field of study.

The trigger for this shift from a cluster of distinct, individual *mathematic* domains to the broad-but-coherent field of *mathematics* was provided by French philosopher, mathematician, and scientist, René Descartes (1596–1650). He developed a way to knit together arithmetic, algebra, analysis, and geometry through the creation of the *x–y* coordinate system that

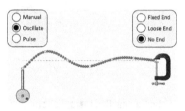

Shaking a string offers another enactive instantiation, and drawing it moves into the space of *iconic* instantiations.

Visit PhET's interactive Wave-on-a-String applet [https://phet.colorado.edu/en/simulation/wave-on-a-string]. **Click on the "Oscillate" and the "No End" buttons to watch the simulated wave action of the string.**

Can you find enough information to graph this sine function? Try graphing it. Notice that both the interactive model and the graph are examples of iconic (image-based) instantiations.

made it possible to use numbers to model locations, distances to model quantities, and equations to model shapes. He also showed how all these constructs could be connected through the same requirement of logical argument. With the masterstroke of the Cartesian coordinate system, the multifaceted and modeling-focused domain of mathematics was born.

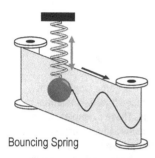

Bouncing Spring

Two familiar enactive instantiations of sine functions can be drawn from the periods of a bouncing spring and a swinging pendulum.

These instances are also good examples of the role of iconic (image-based) instantiations. For most learners, it's not immediately obvious how sine curves figure into the pictures, but well-crafted images can bridge concrete experiences to abstract models.

That means that *mathematics* (as the word is now understood) really isn't that much older than the modern public school. However, and ironically, current mathematics has very little to do with current *school math*. For centuries, school math has moved little while research mathematics has accelerated steadily. Consequently, today's school mathematics bears almost no resemblance to its parent discipline. Such monumentally important (but recent) areas as fractal geometry, complex modeling, network theory, and coding are virtually unrepresented in school math.

An upshot of the ever-widening separation of school mathematics and research mathematics is that many (and perhaps most) people leave high school with an impoverished and disabling view of what the discipline is all about. But, to be fair, it's not that educators haven't noticed the growing gulf. On the contrary, multiple movements over the past 50 years were intended to address it. For example, the "New Math" movement of the 1960s called for a shift in emphasis from mastery of procedures to understanding logical structures and formal propositions – that is, to develop an appreciation for the ways that all branches of mathematics work. The more recent "Reform Math" movement that began in the 1980s was oriented by similar hopes, but somewhat different thinking. Drivers of that reform effort, including the powerful National Council of Teachers of Mathematics (1989), positioned problem solving as a defining quality of all mathematical inquiry, and thus sought to interrupt the entrenched emphasis on rote application of memorized procedures by incorporating unfamiliar situations and challenging puzzles into the mathematics classroom. Another effort to transform school mathematics is now underway. As with previous movements, this "New New Math" revolves around an effort to interrupt

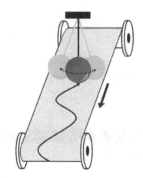

Swinging Pendulum

popular beliefs on the nature of mathematics, and it is also drawing more heavily on recent insights into human learning to challenge popular beliefs on what should be happening in math classes. Consistent with the emerging theories presented in Chapter 2, the movement's foci include extensive use of manipulative tools and multiple representations of concepts, embedded in more collective or group-based structures for inquiring into mathematical processes.

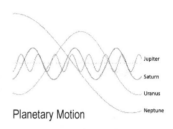

Planetary Motion

Unfortunately, all three of these movements have sputtered. In part, they have been subverted by unrelenting public pressure to prepare learners for standardized examinations and international comparisons that are perceived by many to focus on rote procedures. In part the movements have been frustrated by teachers' tendencies to teach the way they were taught. And in part the shifts have been constrained by a populace that has difficulty appreciating a mathematics education that is different from the one they received. As with any well-entrenched system, school mathematics has proven itself to be highly resistant to change – not because established approaches make sense, but because the momentum of habit is so extreme. Centuries of repetition have supported a material infrastructure (of guides, texts, tests, etc.) and a web of beliefs that are not going to change quickly and that are proving to be resistant to research that shows them to be out of date, ineffective, and otherwise indefensible.

Here are some *iconic* – that is, image-based – instantiations. These examples point to real-world phenomena that can't be experienced directly as periodic functions (mostly because they happen too slowly or too quickly), but that can be readily modeled with sinusoidal functions.

So where is the research pointing?

It might be helpful to know that there have been similar debates involving other school subjects. For example, reading education once focused primarily on helping students learn skills for deciphering symbols and rules for structuring written text. It was assumed that students who could decode sentences would also understand them. But now educators recognize that decoding and comprehension are both necessary elements in a "balanced" approach to teaching reading.

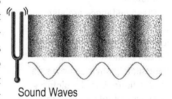

Sound Waves

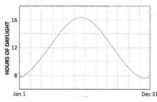

Daylight Hours through the Year

Unfortunately, the idea of balancing doesn't work to resolve the Math Wars. It may appear that one side asserts that schools should focus on teaching technical skills in math while the other believes they should focus on teaching for deep understanding. However,

Moon Phases

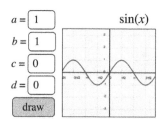

A common symbolic instantiation of the sign function is

$$f(x) = a \sin(bx + c) + d,$$

where *a* is the amplitude, *b* is the frequency, *c* is a translation on the *x*-axis, and *d* is a translation on the *y*-axis.

This form can quickly become meaningul when learners interact with an iconic instantiation based on the formula. For example, the representation offered by the Sine Function HTML5 applet [http://www.analyzemath.com/trigonometry/sine_applet.html] lets you experiment with how changes to *a*, *b*, *c*, and *d* affect the curve.

the sides really aren't that far apart on this issue. Few traditionalists would say that learning math is just a matter of memorizing facts and rules, just as most reformists now recognize that mastery of basic facts and rules is necessary for higher-order thinking. On this count, the sides have compatible intentions. However, challenges arise when discussions shift from *what to teach* to *how to teach*. Educators are often asked to choose between teacher-driven explanations of isolated topics and learner-driven explorations of whole concepts in rich (e.g., problem-based) settings.

Each side seems to have a compelling argument for its view. Proponents of direct instruction assert that mathematics is well-defined and unambiguous, and so it should be delivered efficiently and with fidelity. They argue that it's ridiculous to expect high school students to "discover" concepts that eluded all but the best-prepared minds until quite recently. Advocates of reform counter by noting that learning is not about "acquiring" objects of knowledge. No *thing* passes from teachers' instructions to learners' minds. Rather, learning is about deriving coherent understandings from personal experiences. Thus, presenting mathematics as a purified or standardized form of knowledge risks making it meaningless while suppressing curiosity, creativity, and motivation.

Clearly we're not going to resolve the issue here. But it's important for eduators to be aware of the issues.

Consolidating Key Points

A core assertion in Chapter 2 was that theories of learning are more than simply *descriptions*. They also carry *prescriptions* for teaching – although not always explicitly.

This point is especially evident in the Math Wars. While it is certainly the case that most of the debate revolves around teaching and content, the heart of the disagreement has much to do with beliefs about learning. Based on what we've read, our sense is that traditionalists lean toward folk theories, and reformists tend to invoke constructivist and sociocultural theories.

Search the web for some active debates. Analyze the vocabularies people use to talk about knowing, learning, and teaching. Are we justified in our conclusions?

What is "modeling"?

A "model" is a representation – a description, an image, a copy – that is intended to highlight vital, defining attributes of some phenomenon. A model is a simplification, one that is useful as a tool for understanding.

A "mathematical model" is thus a description of a phenomenon using mathematical constructs. Examples abound, and range from the mundane to the enormously complex. On the more familiar end of the spectrum, every act of counting or measuring is an act of mathematical modeling – that is, of representing a situation in terms of an appropriate number system. The same can be said of topics in high school mathematics, such as the equations generated by Kathy's students to describe their observations of certain types of repetitive and cyclic phenomena. At the more complex end of the spectrum, mathematical models are used in the physical sciences (e.g., physics, chemistry, biology, geology, meteorology, astronomy; see Chapter 6), engineering (see Chapter 5), and the social sciences (e.g., economics, psychology, political science, sociology) to interpret, explain, and predict phenomena that arise in the interactions of many, many agents.

In this sense, since mathematics first cohered into an identifiable domain, the discipline has always been about modeling. In fact, every topic in school mathematics was originally selected for its power to model – and this detail helps to explain why the traditional pedagogical emphasis has been on rote application. In the first public schools, learners were being trained to apply established mathematical models, and to do so efficiently and effectively. Routinized, repetitive instruction that doesn't allow for much divergent thinking is arguably the best way to do that.

But there's a great deal of irony there. The reason that arithmetic and algebra have been at the core of the public school curriculum is that they are such enormously flexible and widely applicable tools of interpretation. Yet they have rarely been taught in a manner consistent with their breadth and power of application. They have been overwhelmingly treated as procedures to be mastered rather than lenses to be polished … calculating rather than modeling.

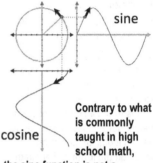

sine

cosine

Contrary to what is commonly taught in high school math, the sine function is not a product of a circle. In fact, it's just as easy to define a circle in terms of two interacting sine curves (one operating vertically, and one horizontally) as it is to define a sine function in terms of a circle – a point that can be demonstrated using dynamic geometry software such as Geometer's Sketch Pad or Cabri. [Wikipedia usually has some excellent dynamic simulations: https://en.wikipedia.org/wiki/Sine]

This chapter's opening anecdote presents an example of how mathematics teaching might look when mathematics concepts are treated as models or lenses rather than just as procedures and calculating tools. To appreciate this point, it's useful to pause to think about things in life that repeat themselves in regular cycles. In everyday life, trigonometric functions are probably the most important examples of periodic functions, and perhaps the most familiar of those is the smoothly undulating sine curve, variations of which appear in many of the margins in this chapter. As illustrated in these margin figures, the sine curve can be used to model a great many phenomena, including changes in daylight hours throughout the year and across different latitudes, moon phases and position on the horizon, ocean waves, planetary motion, sound waves, and electromagnetic radiation. Like other mathematics concepts studied in school, this one is important not because it can be used to answer a textbook question about how high a 5 meter ladder will reach if it forms an 80° angle with the ground (although that's entirely useful!), but because it affords insight into how, for example, making a sound is related to rocking in a boat, playing on a swing, or decreased daylight in winter.

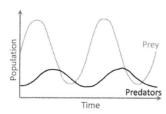

Recently, sine-shaped curves have begun to show up in models of different sorts of population dynamics. For instance, the above graph of the entangled populations of predators and prey presents some interesting features (e.g., they cycle together, but prey population "lags") that have been useful for understanding some of the complexities of the world. (See the "Consolidating Key Points" box on page 47 for more information on this sort of complex modeling.)

The phrasing here is important. Notice that we didn't say that the sorts of phenomena highlighted in these margins are "examples of the sine function." Because they aren't. They are phenomena that can be *modeled* with the sine function – and there's a big difference. The sine function isn't lurking in planetary orbits or sound waves. It is a concept that enables humans to recognize, cluster, and study a particular sort of regularity in the universe. It is a modeling tool.

The vital point here is that mathematics is about humanity's engagement with the world. Concepts are not mined from a mysterious, ideal realm, but are distilled from encounters with many different forms and events. Consider the more familiar concept of multiplication, for example. What is it?

In our experience, most people answer that question with something like "repeated addition" or "a grouping process." In fact, these responses are not definitions. They are only instances or instantiations of multiplication – that is, phenomena that can be modeled using multiplication. Think about, for example, how multiplication can be used to model each of the situations illustrated in the margin on this page.

Each of the illustrated situations can be interpreted as an instance of 2 x 3. They include:

- folding folded paper
- grouping groups
- using a linear function
- making a rectangular array
- compressing a number line
- making combinations (i.e., pairing members of different sets)
- branching branches

Other instantiations include:

- repeated addition
- skip counting
- calculating areas
- scaling (proportional change)
- layering layers
- changing/growing steadily
- adding a dimension.

These lists are only partial. We've counted dozens of distinct instantiations of multiplication in elementary school mathematics alone – and yet curriculum guides and classroom resources are rarely explicit on this range of possibility. We suspect that's because the focus is on mastering calculation rather than realizing the power of modeling. Multiplication is a critical topic to study, not simply because it's a calculating tool, but because it stretches across so many phenomena. It should help learners understand their worlds.

Similar can be said of every topic in school mathematics. That is the insight that Kathy brought to the teaching episode presented in this chapter's opening anecdote. In that classroom, sine functions weren't presented as means to calculate missing side and angle measures on miscellaneous triangles. Rather, they were offered as powerful interpretive tools for identifying and understanding many, many phenomena. Kathy was careful to select instances that can be studied within the constraints of a typical classroom.

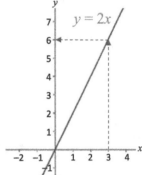

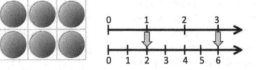

Above and below are several familiar situations that are often modeled using the concept of multiplication.

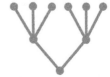

Consolidating Key Points

Complex modeling is a recent branch of mathematical study enabled by inexpensive and abundant calculation power. It focuses on making sense of the collective dynamics of many interacting agents, aiming to answer such questions as "How do anthills 'know' where food is?" and "How do different populations interact when pressed together?"

Several websites offer free multi-agent programmable environments to play around in this branch of mathematics. We recommend the following:

1. John Conway's Game of Life – This simulation is based on just four rules. Add a few populations by clicking on the grid. Play the simulation. What happened to your population?

   https://bitstorm.org/gameoflife/

2. Netlogo – Click on one of their sample models. What is being modeled? How many variables/ rules determine the model? Try changing the variables to see how it affects the model.

   https://ccl.northwestern.edu/netlogo/

3. StarLogo Nova – Create an account to see the models of phenomena that other users have created. Play around.

   http://www.slnova.org/

Another growing area of modeling uses "big data" sets to model patterns, trends and associations. Hans Rosling was a remarkable statistician who made big data meaningful to the general public. We recommend watching any (or all) of Rosling's "top 10 TED Talks."

   https://www.ted.com/playlists/474/the_best_hans_rosling_talks_yo

Hans Rosling's Gapminder provides informative interactive models of the United Nation's massive dataset.

   http://www.gapminder.org

A remarkable finding of this branch of mathematical modeling is that all truly complex phenomena – that is, all systems that adapt and learn, including cells, brains, social groups, bodies of knowledge, and ecosystems – share a similar sort of internal structure. Their elements come together in decentralized networks. This sort of network has no specific center; rather, each node in a decentralized network is, in a sense, the center of its own network. For hundreds of illustrated examples, drawn from art, science, business, linguistics, politics, and other realms, visit:

   http://www.visualcomplexity.com

Summing up

For centuries, school math has been structured around the assumption that mathematics involves rigidly sequenced chains of logical reasoning. Oriented by this principle, for hundreds of years, curriculum developers have been formatting school math as a regimented march through logically parsed knowledge bits.

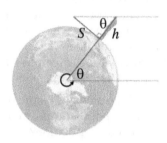

The margin notes in this chapter were intended as a challenge to the beliefs about learning that infuse this deeply entrenched practice. By inviting you to look across multiple instantiations of trigonometric functions and multiplication, we hoped to prompt you to think critically about common school math practices. When you studied sine functions in high school, was the topic connected to pendula, light waves, sound, and other phenomena that might be modeled using sinusoidal curves? When you learned about multiplication, was it used to model folding, grouping, stretching, hopping, and other instantiations? If not, do you think an emphasis on noting and knitting connections among diverse instantiations might have influenced your understandings and appreciations of these mathematical topics?

The issue is not simply a matter of making school math more relevant or interesting. In fact, that's a secondary point. The critical matter, as developed in Chapter 2, is that personal understandings arise as learners see connections across diverse experiences, such as the deep relationship between the profile of a corkscrew and the phases of the moon. Profound mathematical understanding has much more to do with these analogical associations than it does with logical links.

This point has obvious implications for *how* math might be taught. But it also has big implications for *what* is taught. Kathy was teaching much more than is often taught in math class. She not only offered her students a grounding in trigonometric functions (i.e., focused on *calculation*), she was helping them develop mathematical lenses for interpreting their experiences (i.e., focused on *modeling*) – an elaboration that renders school math much more like research mathematics while echoing the original impetus for the discipline.

When we were selecting phenomena to mention in the margin notes for this chapter, one idea that popped up was shadow lengths and how they change throughout the day.

It turns out that this can't be modeled with a sine function, but it can be modeled with a tangent function. The diagrams here are the ones we used to convince ourselves of this point, as they model how the shadows stretch out to infinity in one direction at sunrise, are shortest at mid-day, and then stretch out to infinity in the opposite direction at sunset.

What other phenomena can be modeled with this function?

tan *x*

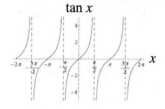

Modeling Challenges

1. Like most recognized knowledge domains, mathematics is divided into many branches or subfields. There is no broad agreement on the number of branches. At the moment (as of October 22, 2018), Wikipedia lists the following main topic areas:

PURE MATHEMATICS	APPLIED MATHEMATICS
• Algebra	• Dynamical Systems and Differential Equations
• Calculus / Analysis	• Mathematical Physics
• Geometry and Topology	• Computation
• Combinatorics	• Information Theory and Signal Processing
• Logic	• Probability and Statistics
• Number Theory	• Game Theory
	• Operations Research

   Again, this list is neither complete nor stable. (In fact, it was significantly reorganized last time we looked.) As well, each category has many subcategories. For example, algebra typically splits into elementary, linear, multilinear, abstract, and other strands.

   Pick three or four of the above strands and do a little research on their foci. As you develop your descriptions, notice how it's easier to characterize each branch in terms of what it *models* than in terms of what it *calculates*.

2. In this chapter's margin notes, we introduced Bruner's (1966) enactive–iconic–symbolic scheme for classifying different instantiations. To recap,

   - enactive instantiations are associated with immediate, bodily experiences,
   - iconic instantiations are based on drawings and images used to interpret experiences, and
   - symbolic instantiations, as the phrase suggests, are represented through abstract symbols.

   This classification scheme comes with advice for teaching. To the extent possible, learners' first encounters with a concept should be based in their actions (enactive). Images, gestures, and other iconic representations might then be used to draw attention to aspects of those actions that are relevant to the concept. As those aspects become more "real" to the learner, symbols can be introduced to label, amplify, connect, and manipulate.

   Identifying, selecting, and sequencing instantiations is not trivial work. This exercise involves highlighting some of the skills that enable this work. Before going too far, though, a few important qualifications are in order.

   Firstly, Bruner's categories aren't hard and fast. Many instantiations fit into more than one category. For example, in which category does the experience of sliding icons around on an iPad belong? It is action oriented (enactive) but image based (iconic) … and very often accompanied by abstract signs (symbolic).

Secondly, the pedagogical sequence of enactive, then iconic, then symbolic is broad advice, not rigid protocol. To that point, some compelling research (e.g., Hiebert & Wearne, 1986) has demonstrated the importance of developing the learner's experiences before pressing into symbol manipulation, but it would be foolish to treat the movement across and through multiple instantiations as a one-way, lock-step process.

Finally, not all instantiations are created equal. Some are simply much more powerful than others for supporting mathematical understanding. In other words, teachers must consider a range of issues when selecting and sequencing instantiations. Some of the criteria we use include:

- familiarity,
- availability,
- usefulness for highlighting specific mathematical principles, and
- ease of mathematical modeling.

These points should come into play in the exercise about *instantiations of "number."*

What's a number?

To an adult's ear, there's a good chance that the above question might sound naïve. But that's not because the answer is trivial; rather, it's more likely because the adult has had decades to assimilate a wide, wide range of very, very different encounters with number. It's a very different story for young learners. And so, a heads-up …

There's a good chance that this task will be confusing and frustrating for you. That's not because you don't understand the topic. In fact, it's just the opposite. It's more likely that you understand it too well. You've probably integrated your experiences so well that instantiations which are wildly divergent might look like they're not different at all.

Step 1: Brainstorm the sorts of things and experiences that numbers are used to represent/model. What are numbers for? What are they used to do?

Step 2: What sorts of simplified images go along with the items that you listed in the previous step? For instance, tally marks or a collection of dots works well for representing the number of people in a room, but they work less well for the numbers used to indicate distances or temperatures.

Step 3: Lakoff and Núñez (2000) identified "four fundamental metaphors of arithmetic" – that is, four principal metaphors for interpreting the concept of number:

- object collection, whereby *number is a count* that models "How many?"
- object construction, whereby *number is a size* that models "How big?"
- measuring stick, whereby *number is a distance* or *length* that models "How far?"
- motion along a path, whereby *number is a position* that models "Where?"

It's easy for experienced knowers to see how these four instantiations of number are alike, but usually more challenging to recognize how they're different. We've found that one effective strategy for making sense of their differences is to imagine how each might be used to illustrate the mathematical statement, "5 > 3." We invite you to think through each case (and perhaps draw images to represent the four different cases) before reading the following paragraph.

With the metaphor of *number as count*, based on object collection, the notion of "greater" means "more objects." For instance, 5 is greater than 3 because there are *more* objects in a set of 5. With the metaphor of *number as size*, based on object construction, 5 is greater than 3 because an object comprising 5 units is *larger* than one comprising three. With the metaphor of *number as length*, based on a measuring stick, 5 is greater than 3 because a 5-unit distance is *longer* than a 3-unit distance. With the metaphor of *number as position*, based on motion, 5 is greater than 3 since it is *farther away* from a common starting point (zero).

How are these alike? How are they different? Can you think of applications where one instantiation makes more sense than others? For instance, which is the most useful – a count, a size, a distance, or a position – for interpreting a grade of 78% on an exam? Which makes sense for converting one currency into another? Which is most useful for making sense of multiplying by π?

We've found that a table like the one below can be a good tool to help think through the different metaphors and images that are at play here.

Grounding Metaphor	Conception of NUMBER	How "5" might look	How "5 > 3" might look	How "5 + 3" might look	How "5 x 3" might look
object collection	count (How many?)				
object construction	size (How big?)				
measuring stick	distance (How long?)				
motion on a path	position (Where?)				

The contents of the table are only a start. What does "+3 + –5 = –2" look like in each case? How do things look across the operations of addition, subtraction, multiplication, division, and exponentiation, and across wholes, rationals, integers, and other sets of numbers? What sorts of confusions might arise for young learners who have developed only the metaphor of *number as count*?

3. Notice that the types of mathematical knowledge needed to engage in the previous exercise is unique to teaching. Shulman (1986, 1987) described it as "pedagogical content knowledge" (PCK), which he defined as

   > ... the most regularly taught topics in one's subject area, the most useful forms of representation of those ideas, the most powerful analogies, illustrations, examples, explanations, and demonstrations – in a word, the ways of representing and formulating the subject that make it comprehensible to others. (p. 9)

   Shulman's "analogies, illustrations, examples, explanations, and demonstrations" fall into the same category as the broader notions of "models," "representations," and "instantiations" used in this chapter. All these words refer to categories of experience and devices used to interpret and connect those experiences.

   Attentive to this point, we prefer to describe PCK in somwhat different terms:

   The teacher is an expert who can think like a novice.

   That is, while it is apparent that educators require subject matter expertise, it's also clear this expertise is different from that of, say, engineers or physicists or mathematicians. One key – and perhaps unique – aspect of teachers' knowledge of mathematics is awareness of diverse instantiations of concepts. Hence, a useful skill among teachers is the ability to deconstruct concepts in ways that give learners access to different interpretations and prompts them toward more nuanced, integrated interpretations and mathematical models of their experiences. (See Davis & Renert, 2014.)

   PCK has been the focus of intense investigation over the past few decades, especially by researchers in mathematics education and science education. We strongly recommend some internet searches (e.g., along the lines of "PCK mathematics education") to get a sense of the importance and breadth of this topic.

Chapter 4

Technology

usage   designing

IN BRIEF

Formal **education** has a history of incorporating new technologies without transforming its aims or strategies. There may be value in embracing the disruptive possibilities of new technologies.

Learners come with different histories and interests. Because their histories are the starting places for new learning, learners will interpret lessons and tasks differently and they will require different sorts of support.

Teachers can and should design tasks in ways that accommodate learner diversity. They can also do so in manners that amplify collective possibilities. Thinking in terms of lesson design (vs. lesson planning) enables possibilities.

Designing Challenges

VIDEO LINK: https://vimeo.com/180805434

Spanning Grades K through 9, Pakan School serves a small, dispersed population in Whitefish Lake 128 First Nation in rural northern Alberta. As with many similar schools in the province, its relative isolation means that students and staff must grapple with many issues that are not major concerns in more urban locales. Regarding curriculum support, for example, the teachers are offered limited professional development and there are no subject area specialists on site. Further, student attendance is often sporadic, owing to such factors as distances, competing interests, and sometimes-low regard for formal education among some members of the community. The sparse population of the area means that the children have fewer opportunities for organized out-of-school activities and very limited access to the educational resources, settings, and experiences that are often taken for granted in more densely populated regions.

When we visited a few years ago, the school had a very traditional feel. The daily schedule was structured around "core" subject areas of language arts, mathematics, and science. For the most part, those classes were organized around textbooks, worksheets, and tests produced by major publishers. There were mixtures of glossy posters and personal touches on the classroom walls, but few indicators of current topics of study and almost no products of student learning.

As for digital technologies, Pakan School was relatively well resourced. Each classroom had four desktop computers and an interactive whiteboard. The school also had a dedicated computer lab and high-speed internet access. With small class sizes between 12 and 18 learners, students had easy and potentially regular access to tools and information. However, uses of these technologies strongly paralleled skills-oriented, utilitarian emphases of core subject areas. Classroom foci tended to revolve around "how to use" programs and applications, framed by direct lessons and well-defined, routinized exercises.

The weeklong robotics workshop, led by a small team of researchers from the university, was thus a break in routine on many levels. Bringing together the Grades 4 and 5 classes into a larger cluster, students were organized into small teams and a problem-based approach was taken to introduce the topics of design and coding. (See Table 4.1 on p. 67 for an overview.) The first session began in a familiar manner, with direct instruction on how to assemble a specific Lego™ robot. But the tone changed abruptly when the initial robots were completed and it came time to code them. Participants were provided with a skeletal introduction to the programming interface and their attentions were directed toward some of the basic commands. They were then invited to program their robots to "dance" by combining forward and backward movements, turns, and noises.

With the shift to this more explorative and collaborative activity, some issues presented themselves immediately. A few students dove in with enthusiasm, but many struggled with the sudden freedom to design their own program, looking to the workshop leaders to tell them exactly what to do. Some teams worked well right away, but it was immediately evident that most students had limited experience sharing ideas and responsibilities around school assignments. Arguments and other tensions quickly arose over materials and tasks.

Other sorts of problems became evident as the tasks became more challenging. At the start of the second session, for example, children were asked to program their robots to trace out regular polygons. Their strategies revealed that they were unable to transfer understandings of measurement, decimal fractions, geometric shapes, multiplication, and other familiar mathematical topics to the tasks at hand. In several instances, for example, teams were unable to resolve the dilemma of "1 unit isn't far enough, but 2 units is too far" – despite the fact that, as their teachers repeatedly reminded them, they had just completed a unit on decimal fractions.

Even so, with minimal direct guidance – coupled with persistent encouragement to embrace challenge, to work together, and to summon previous learnings – the children were soon designing their own robots and taking on complicated coding tasks. As the video clip illustrates, within a few days they were programming their robots to meet the challenge of seeking out and extinguishing fires in a building. In the language of digital engagements, they made the shift from "usage" of technologies to "designing" technologies … and they did so quickly. (See a second video, featuring the winning robot at https://vimeo.com/145404678.)

Consolidating Key Points

What's "technology"?

If you do an image search of the word, you'll get a screenful of graphics like the ones here.

That makes sense. Society is preoccupied with the latest and greatest. But it's important to recognize that there's vastly more to technology than circuits and tablets. Indeed, some have argued that these artifacts aren't even our most powerful technologies. They pale, for example, beside the technologies of language and mathematics.

Look around you. What in your visible range would you classify as technology? What would you not classify as technology?

S**T**EM Education

The past century has seen some remarkable developments in communication and information technologies, including the inventions of motion pictures, radio and television, and (of course) digital computing.

The margin notes in this chapter are concerned with unpacking the episode described in the opening anecdote in terms of key principles of task design.

Formal education has proven to be a keen user of these and other emergent technologies – and, on the surface, it might seem that schools have been keeping pace with these evolutions. However, a comparison of the explosive possibilities of information technologies and the often-prescriptive ways they have been utilized in schools tells a different story. For the most part, innovations have been taken up not to reform or transform what it means to be educated, but to replicate, accelerate, and otherwise amplify entrenched practices and perspectives. For instance, in the first half of the 1900s, some commentators boldly asserted that movies and radio offered the promise of fully standardizing classroom experiences by "teacher-proofing" lessons – that is, ridding the system of inconsistencies in presenting information by offering the same demonstrations and explanations to all learners (Friesen, 2009). Computers were greeted with very much the same mindset in the last half of the 20th century. Rather than challenging or elaborating the educational project, these technologies were mainly taken up as new delivery devices (Cuban, 2003).

One might be justified in thinking that the explosive development of digital technologies in the early 21st century would have forced a different mindset, especially considering the ways that emerging possibilities for accessing information and connecting to one another have transformed the business world and interpersonal relationships. However, like their 20th-century precursors, new digital technologies have been overwhelmingly taken up in schools as means to enhance delivery – for example, using computers for "practice and drilling, and doing individual homework" (OECD, 2015, p. 53), or using interactive whiteboards as enhanced chalkboards. Ironically, rather than advancing or improving schooling experience, "adding 21st-century technologies to 20th-century teaching practices will just dilute the effectiveness of teaching" (ibid, p. 2).

The issues that arise here have to do with both *how* people are taught and *what* they are taught. The individual-focused, explanation-based, practice-heavy emphases of an educational system committed to delivery of information, while still having important roles to play, do not always fit well with emerging realizations on the roles of collaboration and inquiry. With regard to the *what*, as we discuss below, it is clear that the narrow band of literacies captured by the familiar "3 R's" (reading, 'riting, 'rithmetic) falls far short of contemporary possibilities and needs.

In this chapter, then, we engage with the growing realization that emergent technologies can (and should) be used to do more than amplify the project of delivering information. These technologies are transforming society, and so they should be transforming formal education as well. For instance, digital technologies can support a "focus on learners as active participants with tools for experiential learning, foster project-based and inquiry-based pedagogies, and facilitate hands-on activities and cooperative learning" (OECD, 2015, p. 4). We explore these matters in this chapter, focusing on how emerging digital technologies compel reconsideration of what schooling is all about. As illustrated by

Task Design Principle:

COMMON GOAL

Playing in the same sandbox can occasion productive learning.

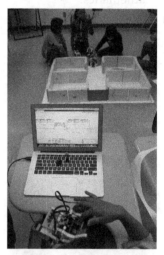

As you view the Pakan video, notice how groups of students are always doing related things, but never identical things.

Choose a single scene. Can you identify the common goal used to define the task? What are some of the variations in student activity? What features of design allow learners to work on different elements at different levels at different paces?

our opening anecdote, for us, the transformations in student agency, collaboration, and utilization of prior learnings that were witnessed over the course of just a week in Pakan School are emblematic of the emerging possibilities for pedagogy. As well, the opportunities to innovate and invent afforded by building and programming robots point to some of the emerging possibilities for curriculum.

For us, these shifts are richly captured in the suggestion that students might be engaged not just in *usage*, but also in *designing*.

Consolidating Key Points

Do a Google Image search of "technology education." How does each image position you? Does it place you more as a user of technology, or as a designer?

Do the same thing for "technology."

What thematic differences do you notice from the previous search. Do these images position you differently?

What is "technology education"?

The word *technology* is often heard as a reference to recent gadgets. Smart phones and radar detectors are obviously technologies. Hammers and highways are less so. But what about languages and literacies?

For some, that's stretching the notion to the breaking point. The opening anecdote for this chapter certainly contributes to the cultural habit of zeroing in on digital devices whenever the word comes up. But we want to pause for a moment and open the discussion a little wider.

The word *technology* traces back to the Proto-Indo-European *teks*, "to weave, fabricate, make," and to the more recent Greek *tekne*, "art, craft, skill" (*O.E.D.*, Weiner et al., 1993). That is, technology is about more than objects and tools; it refers to the ideas, practices, artifacts, and sensibilities that define a culture. Technologies, however, have a habit of growing invisible to us. For instance, while alphabets and numbers were once extraordinary inventions that greatly enabled human thinking, they are now such integral parts of everyday life that it might seem odd to describe them as major technological breakthroughs.

But that's what they were, emergent technologies/arts/crafts/skills that helped to open vast new possibilities for human action.

In a strong sense, then, formal education is (and always has been) focused on becoming familiar with some of a society's more powerful and useful technologies. That was certainly the case in the 18th and 19th centuries, as different nation states settled on the "basics" of literacy and numeracy as the core of the schooling experience. In an era with very low literacy and numeracy rates, providing citizens with access to these technologies was progressive and empowering. Unfortunately, that froze into an unquestioned orthodoxy. To suggest that other technologies – that is, other literacies, skills, and tools – might now rival reading, writing, and arithmetic in importance is often greeted with scorn and derision by "back to basics" advocates.

Perhaps more than any other aspect of the changing world, then, digital technologies are helping to interrupt deeply entrenched beliefs about what and how schools should be teaching. In particular, over recent years there has been a growing recognition that information and communications technologies (ICTs) are major contributors to innovation and economic growth. For instance, the Organization for Economic Cooperation and Development (OECD, 2013) considers computer programming a necessity for a highly skilled labor force. Shortages are already felt across the world and demand for highly skilled ICT professionals is expected to rise. In our home country of Canada, predicted shortages of skilled ICT workers typically hover in the hundreds of thousands – a shortage that is expected to impact ICT innovations and revenues (see Arellano, 2015; Clendenin, 2014).

Canada is hardly unique on this count, as evidenced by major pushes around the world to include program-

Task Design Principle:

MULTIPLE SOLUTIONS

Flexibility in solution processes support creativity.

Review the "Final Robot Co-opetition" (Scene 10) and compare the different water-delivery strategies used by the groups. How were they similar? How were they different?

How were these similarities and differences fostered through the task design?

ming as a core part of school curriculum. In response, some educators and educational systems are shifting emphasis from teaching "how to use" software programs toward "how to code." Estonia and England, for example, have implemented national curricula that make computer programming mandatory for all grades, and other nations appear to be moving in this direction. In Canada, some provinces have developed and implemented mandatory coding curricula. It is currently a topic of political debate in our home province of Alberta. At the time of writing, there are no plans to make coding mandatory, but officials are sending out conflicting signals around the need to provide learners with coding experiences. Things are moving so quickly that we expect this paragraph will be outdated by the time you read it.

Trends toward incorporating programming in school curricula were preceded by a broadly effective worldwide push to get computers in schools. In 2011, 71% of students in OECD countries reported having access to computers and the internet at school. However, most students reported using the computers at school for email, browsing the internet, word processing, or doing individual homework. For the most part, such activities require low-level thinking and do not challenge students to develop more than basic user skills. In contrast, learning how to program a computer involves higher-level cognitive processes and provides opportunities for developing higher-level ICT skills.

Such emphases fly in the face of the ways that digital technologies have been taken up outside of schools. Access to vast stores of information, social networking, crowdsourcing, and online shopping are among the most frequently mentioned uses. But alongside these popular applications, a few cultural movements have emerged that might hint at a significant shift in sensibilities – and, correspondingly, might serve as a prompt for rethinking aspects of schooling. Two of these movements are known as *hacker culture* and *maker culture*.

Hacker culture is the more notorious of the two, given the frequent association of "hacking" with breaching of computer security. While not completely unfair, such

Task Design Principle:

VARIABLE ENTRY

Learners can adapt tasks to fit their knowledge and interests.

Review the "Polygon Task" (Scene 5) and compare the activities of the two groups of learners.

What is the focus for each group? What do they appear to be learning? Which features of the task design support this diversity of engagement?

activities represent only a tiny slice of what hacking is all about. More broadly, hacking refers to all activities concerned with overcoming or circumventing the constraints on systems in order to reach or generate innovative outcomes. That is, hacking isn't always about cheating, but can also be about playful exploration aimed at expanding possibilities. In this sense, a poet's creative use of imagery and metaphor is a sort of linguistic hacking, or a musician's repurposing of household and other items to use as percussion instruments is a sort of acoustic hacking. Hacking, then, isn't defined by the medium (which is usually programming), but by the intentions – namely, pushing out what's possible, doing something meaningful, and developing expertise and excellence.

Maker culture might be described as a more material analog of hacker culture, as it involves very much the same sensibility but is more focused on innovating with physical artifacts. For instance, typical media for "makers" include electronics, robotics, and 3D printing – often coupled to metalworking, woodworking, and other more established arts and crafts. As with hacker culture, there is a strong emphasis on excellence, which in turn involves mastery of practical skills, using proven designs, improving things, and sharing those improvements.

Hacker and maker cultures thus share with traditional schooling a focus on mastery of established knowledge. But they move beyond traditional schooling in the explicit intention to create and innovate – both materially (by, e.g., constructing a robot according to a specific set of parameters) and conceptually (by, e.g., programming it to perform novel tasks). This shift reflects the elaboration used to frame this chapter, in which learners are positioned as more than users (masterers) of technology. They are also designers (participants; contributors).

Shifts in both curriculum content and learner positioning have been accompanied by a growing emphasis on student engagement. The robotics workshop in Pakan School powerfully illustrates this point. Even though the children's prior classroom experiences had overwhelmingly been in the delivery-and-acquisition mode, and

Task Design Principle:

PURPOSEFUL PRACTICE

Practice can be designed to promote mindfulness.

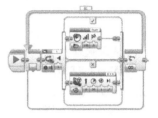

Watch the "Touch Sensors Task" (Scene 6).

The well-defined competency at the center of this task was not easily mastered. Students required several attempts to reach the levels evident in the scene ... and several more afterward before understandings were sufficient to move on to more advanced tasks.

How was the critical concept foregrounded? How was the task designed to encourage reflection? How did the design support iterative (versus incremental) development of understanding?

Task Design Principle:

TASK FEEDBACK

Tasks should provide learners with feedback on their learning.

Review the "Touch Sensors Task" (Scene 6).

Notice how learners were provided with immediate information on their work. Technically, the students were making many errors and enduring repeated failures ... but these "setbacks" served as motivators.

How does immediate feedback reframe "failure"? How does it reframe "success"?

despite the fact that a majority of students greeted the robotics tasks with a "tell me what to do" mindset, for most it took less than a day to engage in ways that were more reflective of hacker and maker cultures.

On that point, and re-emphasizing one of the core themes of this text, it's important to underscore that the move to a more inquiry-oriented attitude did not compromise the traditional components of these children's education. On the contrary, we observed many instances in which the participants applied, consolidated, and extended understandings, in ways that we suspect would never have happened in their more familiar classroom settings. Several examples from mathematics stand out for us. For instance, as mentioned earlier, even though the students had just completed a unit on decimal fractions, many were unable to apply that knowledge when it came to programming their robots to move specific distances or turn through specific angles. And even though each had done hundreds of "timesing questions" in their school careers, not a single person was able to see the path around a regular polygon in terms of multiplication (i.e., repeating a set of actions in a loop) rather than addition (i.e., typing in a sequence of actions over and over). By the end of the week, every student was demonstrating this and many other mathematical competencies in their designs.

Consolidating Key Points

Amy Webb hacked an online dating service.

To be clear, she didn't hack the site. She hacked the service.

Amy explains what she did and why she did it in her TED Talk [https://www.ted.com/talks/amy_webb_how_i_hacked_online_dating].

Have you ever hacked a technology in a similar way? While you might not think of yourself as a hacker, chances are that you've tinkered with or reverse engineered something so that you could exploit it in ways that weren't intended.

Formal education is profoundly resistant to change, in large part because the system is so massive that comprehensive transformation can never happen (Cuban, 2003). But it can evolve as parts are hacked. Identify an element of schooling that you passionately want to see changed. How might you hack it?

What is "design"?

"Design" is one of the most important ideas in current discussions of STEM education, where the word is used to refer to some very specific qualities. Before we lay out what some of those qualities are, let us first flag what design is *not*.

A design is *not* a plan. It is not a scheme that is specified entirely in advance. It is not a rigid step-by-step process that is intended to be performed without deviation. It is not an attempt to predetermine outcomes by anticipating and managing every contingency … none of which is to say that planning isn't an important part of designing …

After all, what does a software designer do? What is an architectural designer up to? What does a clothing designer think about? How might the common elements of these roles help to inform the nature and place of design in formal education?

For starters, designers of buildings, software, and fashion are not focused on dictating what's supposed to happen and they're not preoccupied with achieving narrow, pre-specified outcomes. Rather, they create *affordances* – that is, they open possibilities by defining spaces, structures, and forms. But they don't define what can happen. Effective design doesn't determine what must be done; rather, it attends to what might be done.

Consider, for example, the space that you're in right now. What has it been designed to support? (Perhaps just as relevant: what has the space been designed to suppress?) What are some of the design elements that have been incorporated to do that?

Or think about what you're wearing. What sorts of activities does your clothing support? How does their design contribute to that range of possibilities?

Now think about a "lesson design."

To our analysis, there are two very different meanings of that phrase operating right now. In some settings, "lesson design" is synonymous with "lesson plan," by which a lesson design/plan is interpreted as a script of activity. It is typically parsed into tidy categories of action (e.g., teacher explanation, or student seatwork) that are precisely timed and geared

Task Design Principle:

SOFT SKILLS

Interpersonal skills should be deliberately taught and practiced.

Watch the "Group Dance" (Scene 4), and notice that some students were not participating as fully as others.

Simply telling those students to engage likely wouldn't have helped much. What skill might need further support here? What sorts of practices and ideas might help? How might the task be improved to better include those considerations?

toward meeting prespecified curriculum objectives. That control-oriented interpretation isn't what people had in mind when the idea of design was first imported into education. Quite the opposite, in fact, the notion was intended to interrupt the entrenched assumption that the teacher is supposed to control everything, including student behavior and learning outcomes. Contrary to the plan-based intention of managing what is to happen by scripting activity in advance, the design-based mindset is more possibility oriented (Brown, 1992). In a very similar sense to the way that software engineers or architects format possibilities through their designs, a lesson design should present possibility for movement, to invite the unanticipated, to hack the plan.

This manner of thinking, of course, repositions the student as an active agent rather than a passive recipient. It also reframes knowledge as something more than classroom-based facts and skills. Knowledge can't be inert, externalized facts, but must actually matter in one's world. The purpose of knowing about decimal fractions, for example, is not to do well on textbook exercises and standardized tests, but to apply that knowledge flexibly in situations where it is useful. Of course, few are likely to disagree with that point. Even so, somewhat oddly (and with no evidence that we're aware of), traditional schooling has been operating on the assumption that learners would spontaneously make the leap from routine classroom exercises to meaningful applications. As the children in this chapter's anecdote demonstrated, that leap doesn't always happen. In fact, the evidence suggests the opposite. Without explicit effort, personal learning often does not transfer from one situation to another, even when those situations are highly similar (Bransford et al., 1999).

That's one major reason for moving from planning to designing. A well-designed setting affords ample opportunity for introducing and practicing important facts and skills, but it also affords play, innovation, and invention. Unfortunately, this sort of work doesn't lend itself to the tidy, fill-in-the-spaces template that has long dominated discussions of lesson planning. What

Task Design Principle:

LEARNING TRANSFER

Learnings don't automatically transfer across contexts.

Review the "Moving into the Rooms Task" (Scene 8).
  Many Grade 4/5 math competencies were present in this activity. What are some?* How would you highlight the connections from robotics to mathematics (and vice versa)?

* Note: When we invited teachers to review their curriculum documents to check alignment with mathematics, all but a few objectives were seen to be represented in the task.

can be offered, however, are lists of considerations. Some of ours are below, all of which are developed in more detail in the margin notes in this chapter.

We begin by thinking about the student's experience. Key elements in design-based learning include:

- **COMMON GOAL** – Playing in the same sandbox can occasion productive learning.

- **MULTIPLE SOLUTIONS** – Flexibility in solution processes support creativity.

- **VARIABLE ENTRY** – Learners can adapt tasks to fit their knowledge and interests.

- **PURPOSEFUL PRACTICE** – Practice can be designed to promote mindfulness.

- **TASK FEEDBACK** – Tasks should provide learners with feedback on their learning.

- **SOFT SKILLS** – Interpersonal skills should be deliberately taught and practiced.

- **LEARNING TRANSFER** – Learnings don't automatically transfer across contexts.

- **KNOWLEDGE BUILDING** – Collaborative work is not about doing individual work in group settings, but about making collectives smarter than the smartest in the collective.

- **COMPETENCY-BASED ASSESSMENT** – Benchmarks can provide critical information to teachers.

This list if far from comprehensive – a fact that you might investigate by conducting searches of "task design principles" and related phrases. Had we more margin spaces to fill, additional entries might have included:

- **MODULARITY** – Tasks can sometimes be parsed in ways that don't completely trip up people who miss elements.

- **METACOGNITION** – Plan pauses to reflect and anticipate, attending to learning about learning.

- **ELASTICITY** – Tasks should "stretch," being adaptable for many levels of expertise, ages, and grades.

We could go on, but at this point it seems most sensible

Task Design Principle:

MANAGEABLE CHUNKS

New information should be presented at a measured pace.

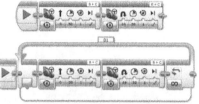

Working memory is very limited and can be easily overwhelmed. Tasks should thus be formatted so that learners have opportunities to practice and consolidate meaningful aspects as they work toward broader skills and understandings.

Choose a pair of sequential scenes. What skills were being developed in the first scene, and how were they iteratively elaborated in the second? How were the subtasks designed to scaffold this development?

Task Design Principle:

KNOWLEDGE BUILDING

*The collective can be smarter
than the smartest in the collective.*

**In the Chapter 6 margin notes,
we present some principles of
"Knowledge Building," a way
of looking at how knowledge is
collectively generated.**

**These principles address in-
terpersonal dynamics, but they
can also be seen as elements of
task design. Preview the notes
and pick a few principles to use
in analyzing a scene from the
Pakan video. How might they be
used to inform the design?**

to pause with an acknowledgement that such lists can be more debilitating than empowering, especially in preliminary stages of designing tasks that are appropriate for a particular discipline and fitted to specific students. We thus see them more as iterative elements in the design process. That is, we do not see the items on the previous page as a fixed list of requirements that must be checked off when designing a lesson, but as an evolving set of considerations that are revisited as tasks unfold. None of the items can ever be "completed"; each can always be improved.

That said, one of the elements on the list merits special emphasis: SOFT SKILLS. An argument that is growing louder and more common in educational circles is that technologies are evolving so rapidly that schools should consider paying much more attention to supporting interpersonal competencies than to developing technical proficiencies. As this argument goes, tools will soon be available that will render hard-won technical proficiencies largely irrelevant – whereas social competence will always be useful. Classrooms provide important opportunities for the development of social skills under an adult's guidance, and this fact may be of mounting importance as digital technologies press deeper and deeper into social interactions. To this end, strategies intended to support the development of soft skills typically revolve around the following sorts of questions: How will students be drawing on one another's insights? What sorts of opportunities will they have to negotiate responsibilities, to settle disputes, to honor differences, and so on? Are competitive elements of the task balanced with expectations to cooperate? How might an over-arching sense of a collective project be encouraged and sustained?

With these considerations in mind, it's important to remember that most lessons will include both highly structured sections and much more explorative elements – and everyone has seen parts of lessons that push too far in one direction or another. In one of our early robotics workshops, for example, participants were given no freedom. They were told which robot to build and which commands to enter. In this case, few participants developed the confidence and competence to design their own robots by the end of the activity. In another instance, students in a "gifted" program were simply given kits and invited to assemble and program their own robots (on the assumption that it was insulting to tell a gifted learner what to do). In this case, even after many sessions of trying, few participants managed to assemble a functional robot, much less to program it to meet the sort of challenge we like to pose (and that the Pakan students met in just a few days).

One session was too directive and rigid. The other was too undefined and loose. Finding that balance between highly structured, regulated activity and more fluid, explorative activity is perhaps the trickiest aspect of effective design. In fact, it is nearly impossible if the conditions listed above aren't considered.

To illustrate some of these points, we turn now to a brief overview of our own lesson design for our robotics workshop. The workshop design for the Pakan School was structured around a series of six increasingly complex tasks spread out over four days. As outlined in Table 4.1, each task extended previously learned skills as it afforded increasing independence in the design process.

This initial design was developed using the principles of Common Goal, Multiple Solutions, Variable Entry, Purposeful Practice, Task Feedback, Soft Skills, Learning Transfer, Competency-Based Assessement, and Knowledge Building, as described earlier and as highlighted in the margin notes of the chapter. What's missing in this table is a sense of the complex, adaptive processes that must be present in every moment of teaching. Phrased differently, and re-emphasizing a core principle of this chapter, a *design* is not a *plan*. It is not an itinerary to be slavishly followed; it is not a list of to-do's that must be checked off. A design is a thought experiment, and it should never serve as a substitute for or an impediment to direct and immediate engagment with learners' emerging understandings. To get a sense of the relationship between initial design and lived design, it would be more informative to compare Table 4.1 with this chapter's opening anecdote and the accompanying video.

Task Design Principle:

COMPETENCY-BASED ASSESSMENT

Benchmarks can provide critical information to teachers.

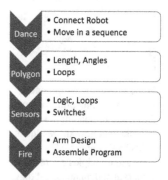

Rewatch the entire video of the Pakan episode, following along with the information provided in Table 4.1 (on the facing page).

For each entry in the "Key Required Understandings" column, identify the sorts of evidence that might be used to assess emergent competencies. Are appropriate benchmarks present? If not, how might you tweak the task design?

Table 4.1: An overview of the task design of the Pakan robotics activity

	Task/Challenge	Key Required Understandings
Day 1	Build the robot in the instruction booklet	• Interpret 2D images to select, orient, and combine 3D objects.
	Program the robot to dance.	• Master necessary technical skills, such as connenting robotics and downloading programs. • Code by selecting and assembling sequences of motor programming blocks. • Use loops (versus entering the same sequence) to program repeated actions.
Day 2	Without using sensors, program the robot to trace out a regular polygon.	• Relate length of a polygon side to robot's wheel rotations by estimating measurement and movement. • Relate angle of polygon to robot's wheel rotations by estimating measurement and movement. • Translate measurements into programming code to move a robot specific distances through specific angles. • Use a loop program for the robot to trace out a regular polygon.
	Using the touch sensor, program the robot to stop and turn when encountering an obstacle.	• Apply IF-THEN logic to program the robot to discriminate when robot touches an object. • Use a loop and switch so the robot will respond to obstacles in path to continue moving.
	Using an ultrasonic sensor, program the robot to stop and turn when encountering an obstacle	• Apply IF-THEN logic to program the robot to discriminate how close it approaches an object • Code using a loop, a switch block and movement blocks so robot will respond to obstacles in path to continue moving without touching the object.
Day 3	Program a robot to seek out and extinguish a fire (or fires) in a four-room building	• Design and assemble an arm or attachment for the robot that can carry water (blue pompoms) and unload them at the appropriate location. • Design and assemble a program that enables the robot to move into a specific room, check for fire, douse the fire if appropriate, and repeat the process for each of the other three rooms.
Day 4	Robot co-opetition	• Share and celebrate the group's accomplishment with the robot's capabilities. • Communicate the capabilities of the robot to peers.

Consolidating Key Points

Find some "lesson plan" templates on the internet. Most of these will divide the lesson into several main blocks – typically:

- Review and/or Orientation
- Main Lesson
- Guided and/or Independent Practice
- Closure

Contrast the elements of this sort of plan with the overview provided in Table 4.1 (on the previous page). How are they the same? How are they different?

Summing up

We selected our experiences at Pakan school as the illustrative case in this chapter for many reasons. Most obviously, the events there are useful for highlighting the nature and role of design in both the work of the teacher and the learning tasks of the students.

Regarding both those design elements, we'd like to close the chapter by recounting an unexpected tension among students that arose soon after they were introduced to the challenge of designing a robot that could detect and extinguish a fire. Within a half hour of hearing about the task, one group designed, assembled, coded, and tested an arm-like appendage that could toss water (i.e., blue pompoms) to the side. And, unsurprisingly, that quick success prompted many of the other groups to mimic the design.

While we continued to encourage those other groups to think independently and to try to come up with their own distinct designs, we weren't troubled by the tendency to copy many of the features of a successful model. Copying is, after all, something that happens across most domains of human activity. However, most of the students – and especially the ones who invented the water-tossing arm – saw things differently. To them, copying the arm was cheating. In fact, just looking at the arm was taken as an affront at first.

The event was a powerful reminder of the complexity of teaching. It foregrounded for us that supporting

Task Design Principle:

PRIORITIZING LEARNING

Technologies should serve learning, not vice versa.

If your were asked to help choose a kit for use in a robotics workshop, what sort of critiera would you suggest.

Look online to learn more about different candidates (e.g., Cubetto, Sphero, Arduino, EZ-Robot, or virtual robots such as Scratch). Why might EV3 robots have been chosen for the Pakan workshop?

the development of soft skills is as important as teaching the hard skills that are specified in curriculum documents. That is, it highlighted that teaching is never a simple matter of using a resource or implementing a pre-planned sequence of activities. Teaching is always about designing – about blending the anticipated with the emergent, the planned with the unexpected, the required with the possible.

The core theme of this chapter – that is, that learners might be positioned not just as users, but as designers in technology education – is thus an idea that applies just as well to teachers. Teachers are not simply users of resources or implementers of programs. They have no choice but to be designers in their classrooms.

Designing Challenges

1. As just mentioned, the principles of design discussed in this chapter are not only about technology; they also apply to teaching. In fact, they're relevant to every aspect of human experience.

   We've used them as we crafted each of the tasks in this book. We invite you to look back at the trigonometry task in the opening anecdote in Chapter 3. How was variable entry embodied in the task? That is, how did the task provide appropriate challenges for students with varied levels of competence in trigonometry? What sorts of feedback mechanisms were implicit in the activities? How did the task design support transfer? Were students compelled to practice key skills and concepts as they worked through different activities? How did they make their new insights explicit? What demands did the task place on their interpersonal skills, and how might it have supported the development of those skills?

2. Pick a Tutorial on the Scratch Project page [https://scratch.mit. edu/projects/editor/?tip_bar=home] and complete it.

   The projects on the Scratch Project page are intended to help you learn and use a programming language, but do they involve you as a designer? Analyze the task you completed according to the key features of design introduced in the chapter (i.e. Common Goal, Multiple Solutions, Variable Entry, Purposeful Practice, Task Feedback, Soft Skills, Learning Transfer, Knowledge Building, and Competency-Based Assessement).

3. As mentioned a few times in this chapter, one of the surprises in our Pakan experience was that students initially had very poor facility with decimal concepts, even though they had just completed a unit on the topic in math class. Other concepts that had also been studied in math class – and that didn't seem

to transfer well – included properties of regular geometric shapes, principles of measurement, and decomposing tasks into logical sequences.

As also noted in the chapter, that sort of happening isn't entirely unusual. Humans do not automatically transfer knowledge developed in one setting to demands encountered in another, even when those situations are highly similar.

As workshop leaders, we were caught off guard, and so our tasks and explanations to support transfer of learning between math and robotics were invented on the fly. Imagine that you've been invited to lead a similar workshop, but (unlike us) keenly aware that you can't assume that critical mathematical skills will transfer readily. How might you tweak task designs (in math class and/or the robotics workshop) to support transfer? Pick one of the mathematics topics mentioned in the first paragraph of this question and design a task sequence that might support transfer – and, in the process, support richer and more robust understandings in both settings.

Chapter 5

Engineering

application   innovating

IN BRIEF

Compared to the other STEM domains, engineering doesn't get much airplay in **education**. That's ironic. It's the most influential – materially, conceptually, and economically.

Necessity and challenge are powerful motivators of **learning**, especially when learners are supported in the iterative cycle of asking–imagining–planning–creating–testing–improving.

Teaching learners' to innovate involves balancing requirements to think about key concepts, to play with ideas and materials, and to embrace failure as a site of learning.

Innovating Challenges   VIDEO LINK: http://galileo.org/catapult-engineering/

Constructing catapults is a popular classroom activity, for lots of reasons. From the vantage point of educators, catapults present opportunities to study and apply many curriculum topics – including, for example, force, trajectories, and properties of simple and complex machines (Alberta Education, 1996, 2014). From the perspectives of students, they're simply fun to build and even more fun to test.

Effective use of the activity in a science unit, however, is not a simple matter of inserting a "build a catapult" objective into a unit on mechanical systems. As Nicole noted, without careful design of this sort of learning activity, it is unlikely to provide sufficient opportunity for students to apply understandings of key concepts. Conversely, many possibilities for both learning and applying emerging insight open up with careful attention to background knowledge and deliberate incorporation of principles of the engineering design process into the learning activity.

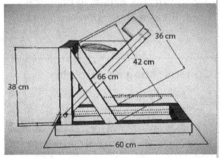

As Nicole demonstrated in her unit design, combining scientific principles with the engineering design process isn't a simple matter of layering bits of science and bits of engineering. Rather than presenting key topics as separate chunks of information, the catapult activity afforded Nicole the opportunity to blend discussions of core concepts with discussions of engineering design.

She began the inquiry with a video of a catapult (or, more specifically, a trebuchet) in action. She then tasked her Grade 8 students with designing a catapult that could throw a tennis ball a distance of five meters. Once students had initial design plans in place, Nicole introduced them to the classes of levers found in the six types of simple machines. With this new information on which class of lever would best suit their catapult, students were asked to revise their initial plans. The unit unfolded with lessons on work, force, distance, and mechanical advantage, sponsoring opportunities to think about how they might improve the distance and accuracy of their throws. Designs were revised and finalized.

Next, with the help of online tutorials, students used Google Sketchup to draw high-quality, to-scale blueprints – an activity that helped to improve designs even

more as it highlighted issues in measurement and other easy-to-overlook considerations. Once the blueprints were done, the building happened, leading up to a culminating throwing competition. One catapult threw the tennis ball over 100 feet. Several others were precise enough to hit the same target three times in a row.

Throughout the unit, Nicole helped her students attend to how engineering a catapult was a process of applying the scientific principles they were studying. She also highlighted how engineering was more than application; considerable innovation was also needed to meet unanticipated problems and challenges.

Check out the site's video links to learners' activities. Notice how they're applying important scientific principles ... but also notice the purpose of those *applications*: they're about *innovating*.

Consolidating Key Points

Look into the history of the word *engineering*. What are its origins? When was it coined? What might its original meanings reveal about its foci, its role in society, its evolution as a field, and so on? (Hint: The catapult activity fits well with the original meaning of *engineering*.)

For a more generous and encompassing account of what engineering is all about, check out this video:
https://www.youtube.com/watch?v=bipTWWHya8A.

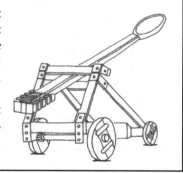

ST**E**M Education

While we might quibble with the definitions that different people attach to the words "mathematics," "science," and "technology," it's clear that these terms are familiar and meaningful to almost every citizen of the western world. For the most part, no one asks "What does that word mean?" when one of them is mentioned.

That's not the case with the word "engineering." In our experience, relatively few people are familiar with what engineering is all about; and most of those who are willing to offer some sort of definition tend to tilt toward descriptions such as "problem solving" and "applied science."

Such descriptions aren't wrong, but neither are they particularly useful to answer the "What is engineering?" question. On the positive side of things, they signal that engineering is concerned with "real" problems and that engineering involves "real" science. Regarding types of problems, engineering aims to address real-world concerns and needs – problems that are situated, that may well be moving targets, and that likely demand new sorts of thinking. To the matter of *applied* science, engineering draws deliberately on evidence-based knowledge – proven insights into the strengths of materials, the interactions of substances, the structures of various forms, and so on.

As this chapter unfolds, you might notice that the words *engineering* and *design* (as discussed in the previous chapter) have overlapping meanings. Indeed, they aren't two different things. Engineering isn't a remote and esoteric domain; it is an area of human engagement that is present in virtually every aspect of your experience. Take a moment to think about what you're looking at right now. That artifact's design – whether it's a book, a piece of paper, a computer screen, or another means of representing print – is a feat of engineering. It is the result of multiple iterative processes of asking–imagining–planning–creating–testing–improving. That is, it's the result of many layers of engineering. Sitting behind something as simple as a sheet of paper are developments and innovations

Engineering Design Elements

This chapter's sidebars deal with using elements of engineering design as strategies to prepare for teaching.

across centuries of mechanical, chemical, and other engineering domains.

A clue as to what engineering is all about just emerged in that last sentence. In the worlds of professional engineers, the word is never encountered alone. Rather, one is a software engineer, or a civil engineer, or a genetic engineer, or a mechanical engineer, or an aerospace engineer, or an electrical engineer, or a geomatics engineer, or a systems engineer, or …. The list goes on. Such lists reveal that engineering, whatever the branch, is rooted in deep scientific knowledge of a domain, and that engineering is about applying that knowledge in ways that meet needs and address concerns. So popular descriptions such as "problem solving" and "applied science" are entirely fitting.

At the same time, however, such descriptions aren't entirely satisfying. To our ear, they have a flavor of "Find a hole; fill it; move on." But as we pause to gaze at the space we inhabit right now, it's obvious that engineering has done much more than apply some science to solve some problems. Through its contributions to the materials used to construct the things around us, the designs used to combine those materials into stable structures, the devices used to record our observations, the smart phones in our pockets that keep distracting us from our work … (we really could go on and on for some time with these lists!), it is evident that engineers do more than solve problems through *application* of science. They are also *innovating*; engineering is all about constantly pushing out the bounds of possibility.

Engineeing Design Element 1:

ASKING

Was the catapult task a "good" engineering education problem? That is … did it involve multiple considerations and demands? If so, what are those considerations? Was there an ideal solution to the problem? Was there a material outcome? Was the task conceptually demanding? Was it more than an academic exercise?

Consolidating Key Points

Visit the webpages of the engineering department of a nearby university. What programs are offered?

At our home institution, the University of Calgary, the following subdomains are listed: Biomedical, Chemical, Civil, Computer, Electrical, Geomatics, Manufacturing, Mechanical, Mechatronics, Oil and Gas, Petroleum, Structural, Software, Transportation. This list is highly reflective of the Calgary economy. Is that the same for the list of subdomains for universities near you?

UNIVERSITY OF CALGARY

SCHULICH
School of Engineering

What is "engineering education"?

Engineeing Design Element 2:

IMAGINING

How did Nicole sponsor the student's initial imaginations of their catapult? What tools did she provide them? What ideas did Nicole wish to convey? How did she monitor students' ideas? What do you suppose she might have adapted to students' emerging needs and learning?

Before we move too far into this section, it's probably important to flag that, in the academic world, the phrase "engineering education" has a specific meaning. As might be predicted, it is most commonly used to refer to post-secondary studies in engineering. Given this book's interest in the K–12 experience, we are thus keen to make it clear that we're not using the phrase that way here.

The fact that we feel compelled to highlight that detail is telling. In particular, it underscores a point made at the start of the previous section, that unlike the other domains under the STEM umbrella, engineering is a somewhat foreign notion to most people. That probably shouldn't come as much of a surprise, given that "engineering education" isn't typically seen to be part of the grade-school experience.

This observation serves as the backdrop for this section, where we wonder aloud how engineering education might look in institutions and at grade levels that have so little experience with and knowledge of the enterprise. Building on the previous section, we organize this one around a pair of subthemes: *engineering as problem solving* and *engineering as applied science*.

Engineering (education) as problem solving (education)

How might toothpaste be packaged in a manner that protects and preserves it, makes it easy to apply to toothbrushes, and is economical? How might smartphone interfaces be organized so that users can quickly access what they want, move fluidly between applications, and accommodate a great variety of uses? How might a community be structured to enable easy flow of people, minimize consumption of fossil fuels, and yet feel expansive and afford welcoming recreation spaces?

It's unlikely that many readers have grappled with these sorts of questions – and the very fact that they haven't been compelled to do so is testimony to the intelligent and highly effective work of different groups of engineers. On this count, good engineering is like good housekeeping. You usually don't notice it when it's done, but you always notice it when it isn't. Ironically, then, good engineering can be hard to see. It's evident in such easy-not-to-notice qualities as seamlessness of experience, ease of use, and range of options. That is, the best engineering fades into the background so that the actual using, doing, and living are eased and enriched. On this point, we invite you to inspect your surroundings (assuming you're not in the middle of a forest). The wall paint, the building materials underneath that paint, the chair you're sitting on, the computer application you're using, the fan that's circulating the air, and so on – these engineered elements are not usually present to consciousness. Yet they format what is possible and likely. Engineers, both literally and figuratively, shape the world.

That shaping happens around solving of problems – where, critically, problems always seem to arrive in the plural. Toothpaste containers, smartphone interfaces, and community plans typically arise in the negotiation of multiple needs, diverse constraints, and frequently conflicting expectations. This is an important preliminary consideration for engineering education. What sorts of problems might be posed that both invite participants to assess an appropriate range of factors and don't overwhelm them with too many considerations?

We think that the catapult engineering task mentioned at the start of the chapter is a good example of an activity that strikes an appropriate balance. It compels young participants to think across matters of form and function, in a manner that permits sufficient and informative levels of success. It also affords them opportunity to be attentive to the specific conditions of a different world, which includes a wide array of possibilities and constraints that they would not normally be compelled to consider.

Further to the topic of qualities of "good engineering education problems," we would like to propose the following as a preliminary list of foci:

- Involves multiple considerations/demands (i.e., likely involves compromise)
- Compels attentiveness to the context (i.e., is situated)

Engineeing Design Element 3:

PLANNING

The design process isn't a linear sequence. Rather, it is iterative, involving multiple iterations of every element.

In fact, each of *those* elements is iterative. Look at the way that students' catapult plans were developed in the catapult unit. How was the process iterative? Why might Nicole have structured things that way? How did that structure intersect with the learning goals of the unit?

- Does not have a "perfect" solution (i.e., invites improvement)
- Has a material outcome (i.e., is more than an academic exercise)

Regarding the entries on this list, we find the graphic below (Figure 5.1) to be particularly useful as we think through possible prompts and problems for engineering education. An engineering problem is, by definition, an invitation to create – but to create in a manner that is attentive to needs, established knowledge, and situational constraints. That means that design and construction likely cannot happen in two discrete phases. Rather, engineering is an iterative process of contemplating and making as one gradually homes in on possibilities that provide sufficient solutions to the original problem.

Figure 5.1. A visual metaphor for the design–construction transition

And, of course, the problem and problem solving may well not end there. Newly engineered solutions to old needs and concerns often introduce, trigger, and / or cause whole new categories of unanticipated issues. Especially over the last half century, with recognitions of climate, energy, and other growing concerns, this realization has sponsored an important evolution in the domain. Engineering and engineering education are not just responsive fields, focused mainly on solving existing problems. They are also responsive fields, attending to the consequences – intended and unintended – of their solutions.

Engineering (education) as applied science (education)

In many universities and technical schools, the terms "engineering" and "applied sciences" are used interchangeably. A quick review of some of the academic topics addressed in this chapter's opening anecdote provide some insight as to why this might be the case. By way of a starting list, here are a few of the concepts invoked in the catapult task:

- Mathematics
  - measurement (e.g., length/distance, angles)
  - proportional reasoning (e.g., scale diagrams)
  - shape (e.g., parabolas)

- Physics
  - simple machines
  - force
  - energy conversion
  - ballistics and trajectories

Engineeing Design Element 4:
CREATING

Nicole scaffolded students' understandings as they moved back-and-forth between the study of scientific concepts and the application of those concepts in their designs. Such scaffolding is useful for appreciating what engineering education is all about. Firstly, engineering education is a domain unto itself. It shouldn't be seen as a vehicle to smuggle scientific concepts into the curriculum, but as a site to engage with those principles in a manner fitted to the task at hand. Secondly, as educational and cultural psychologist Jerome Bruner (1960) famously asserted, "any subject can be taught effectively in some intellectually honest form to any child at any stage of development" (p. 33). Phrased differently, it is possible to engage authentically with topics such as force and acceleration without speedometers and formulas. In fact, such preliminary, informal engagements may be critical to the development of more powerful conceptual understandings later in one's schooling career. As discussed in Chapter 2, contemporary cognitive science research has highlighted that understandings of even the most abstract formulations are rooted in bodily activity as humans maneuver through, manipulate, and otherwise experience a physical world (Lakoff & Johnson, 1999). An immediate upshot of this realization is that engineering tasks should be selected and designed so that students have engaged physically – and that they be made aware of how these experiences relate to scientific and engineering concepts.

To create their catapult, students brought materials from home. Who decided which materials were appropriate? How was that decided?

Students spent one day in the Industrial Arts room to complete most of the build. What would Nicole have had to think about there?

It rarely works out, especially when working with larger groups, that all the creating happens within the space and time set aside for creating. What sorts of strategies might be put into place to accommodate?

A further implication is that, like work in all STEM domains, work in engineering should be understood as an iterative process. This point has been captured by many commentators in looping diagrams intended to represent some aspects of the process. The image repeated in this chapter's margin notes represents our efforts to collect and consolidate many of these elements into our own model.

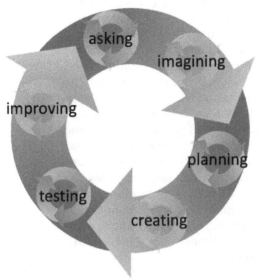

Figure 5.2. One representation (of many possibilities) of iterative engineering processes

As with any such diagram, the point of this one is more to invite readers to consider the range of activities that might be involved in an engineering task than it is to suggest that the list of elements is exhaustive or appropriately sequenced. The fact of the matter is that, as with any creative human endeavor, the processes involved in any actual engineering task are unlikely to follow such simplistic representations.

Recapping this section's important points: within an engineering task, it is important that participants are oriented toward the science at hand. Often, but not always, such orientation involves pausing to study established scientific principles. Frequently, it is quite acceptable just to apply – that is, to draw on others' intellectual heavy-lifting by using a formula and starting with a device that can be used opportunistically in the application at hand.

At the same time, it would be inaccurate to suggest that engineering is mainly about applying insights developed elsewhere by others. Engineering is an inherently creative process, and engineers have made massive material, conceptual, and economic contributions. Regarding material innovations, as already emphasized, our worlds are formatted by artifacts and processes designed by engineers. Conceptual innovations are just as broad and impactful – and especially obvious in this digital era. Engineers have contributed immensely to conceptual advances in mathematics, science, and technology, with particularly notable contributions over the last century. For example, in the branch of study known as "information science," many discipline-defining contributions have come from engineers. As for economic innovations, one need only mention such multinational powerhouses as Ford Motors and Apple. Science might have provided the foundational insights, but engineering developed them in ways that transform and define entire economies.

Once again, then, engineering is clearly much more about innovating that application. But what, exactly, is meant by "innovation"?

Consolidating Key Points

Search for images of "engineering process" and any related phrases that you might be able to think of. Compare the search results to the model we offered in this chapter's margin notes. Did we miss something important? Did we over- or under-emphasize some key aspect? Are other models more compelling to you? Elaborate.

As you consider these questions, if might be useful to do a search for "engineering design competitions" to get a sense of the types of challenges that are typically set for engineering students. Do models of the engineering process, such as the one offered in Figure 5.2, help to illuminate some of the decisions that oriented instructors as they designed those tasks?

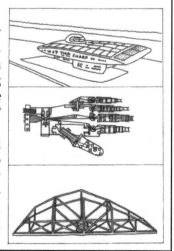

What is "innovation"?

Is the smart phone an "invention"? Or is it an "innovation"?

This distinction is an important one, especially when it comes to engineering. Often engineering is cast in terms of *invention* – that is, of creating an artifact or process for the very first time. That certainly happens, but invention is more the exception than the rule. Most engineering is more a matter of *innovation* – that is, improving, elaborating, adapting, combining, or otherwise hacking existing artifacts or processes in ways that expand their possibilities or open them to new uses.

Engineeing Design Element 5:

TESTING

Notice that testing the catapult was done repeatedly throughout the unit. What were the purposes of the repeated testing? How was the testing conducted? Formally? Informally? Small groups? Whole class? Why would Nicole have chosen the format for this testing? What learning goals did Nicole interject into the teaching? How did Nicole use the testing opportunities for teaching those learning goals? How did students record and analyze the results of their testing?

The smartphone falls into this latter category. It's an innovation, and this point becomes obvious when its range of uses is considered. Here's a partial list of how we've used ours over the past 24 hours:

- clock
- calendar
- calculator
- game center
- remote control
- camera
- video display
- photo album
- text and email device
- global positioning system
- internet portal
- payment tool
- hard drive
- activity/fitness monitor
- thermostat
- garage door opener

Oh yes. And telephone. Clearly there is invention behind each of these applications. That is, someone (or, more likely, a group of someones) invented the clock, the camera, the internet, … and of course the microprocessors and the coding that are needed for each of the entries on this list. But the emergent product of the smart phone isn't an invention in this sense. It's an innovation – and sometimes frustratingly so for those who are keen to keep up with the latest and greatest tools.

We could say much the same thing about mountain bikes, the concrete used to build skyscrapers, gel pens, and Angry Birds. All these examples are based on inventions (of, e.g., levers, wheels, self-hardening mixtures of clay and crushed limestone, the sticks used to gouge clay tablets, and coding languages). But there are long lineages of engineering innovation between the original inventions and the current forms.

It's impossible to offer an all-encompassing description of what is involved in innovation, in part because
the word encompasses a broad range of processes that
are simultaneously emulative and creative, and orderly
and disruptive. We've gathered some of these processes together in Figure 5.2, in which we've attempted
to highlight that innovation is at least as much about
attending to what has already been accomplished as
it is about endeavoring to push out the boundaries
of what's possible. In fact, it is this simultaneous attentiveness to both established accomplishments and
emergent possibilities that distinguishes invention
from innovation – and which, correspondingly, has
prompted so many commentators to suggest that humanity has evolved out of an "era of invention" into
an "era of innovation" (e.g., Bhasin, 2012).

We invite you to consider Figures 5.1 and 5.2 as a
sequence of more finely grained analyses of the engineering process. A more "complete" model of the co-
entangled processes involved in engineering emerges
as the loops in the problem-solving trajectory (Figure
5.1) are understood as instances of the iterative process of applying science, within which are embedded
multiple cycles of innovation (Figure 5.2).

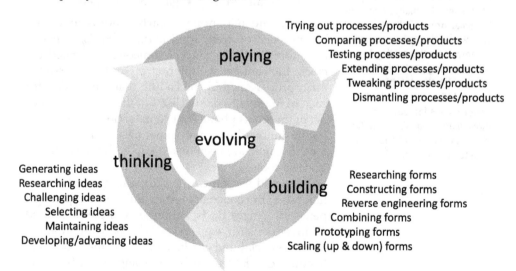

Figure 5.2. One representation (of many possibilities) of
the multiple processes associated with innovating

We also invite you to revisit the catapult activity described in this chapter's opening anecdote and consider the different processes of innovation involved. When and how might learners draw on already-consolidated knowledge? When and how might they introduce their own ideas? When would thinking be the focus? Playing? Building? How might these activities intertwine and cycle together? How are possibilities enabled, amplified, frustrated, and or suppressed through expectations of and opportunities for collective activity?

Engineeing Design Element 6:

IMPROVING

How many opportunities were students given to improve the design? When were the students given opportunities to improve their design? Where were the opportunities for improvement provided? How did Nicole ensure that students used reasoned judgments and not simply trial and error to improve the design?

While such activities can never be fully specified in advance, teachers must consider these sorts of questions throughout the process of designing engineering tasks for their classrooms. It's easy to throw them into imbalance. For example, borrowing a catapult kit from a library will likely focus attentions on playing but dramatically constrain both thinking (e.g., students don't need to design) and building (e.g., snapping things together replaces crafting and assembling parts). Similar can be said of lesson designs from popular websites. Pre-packaged activities and canned lessons are much less likely to compel students to work through the conceptual and pragmatic implications of concepts under study. Unbalanced combinations of thinking, playing, and building can trigger frustrations for all involved.

With regard to these sorts of elements, the act of structuring a lesson might appropriately be described as an act of engineering. It is about problem solving, insofar as every lesson is intended to address a perceived need. It is about applied science, insofar as every teaching event should be informed by evidence-supported insights into how humans learn, what's important to know, and so on. Every lesson is an opportunity for innovation, as the familiar and the tried-and-true are considered against the inevitable novelty represented among interests and expertise of class participants.

We would actually take the metaphor of "structuring a lesson is an engineering process" one step further. As emphasized throughout the chapter, engineering is rarely about assembling existing parts into a new whole. Most often it involves some manner of disruptive innovation – that is, of challenging entrenched habits of thinking and interrupting established patterns of acting. While not every act of problem solving requires disruptive innovation, as Albert Einstein famously reminded, "We can't solve problems by using the same kind of thinking we used when we created them." That is, the obstructions that prevent a system from finding solutions to its current dilemmas are often self-imposed. They conceal themselves as mental models, assumptions, routines, and so on. These living constraints can be the main reason for preserving things as they are and frustrating attempts to engineer new, fitting, and powerful solutions – even in the face of great crises.

The prominent role of disruptive innovation in the engineering process also helps to make sense of the highly collaborative and interactive nature of the field. It's not an accident that engineering competitions always involve teams. One reason for the team-based emphasis is that the specific categories of expertise needed to address a problem can't always be predicted in advance, and a team affords a greater range of proficiencies. Arguably, however, a more important reason is that it's much, much harder for individuals on their own to be aware of the beliefs and practices that may be preventing the emergence of useful new insights.

Engineeing Design Cycle:

ASKING•IMAGINING•PLANNING •CREATING•TESTING•IMPROVING

Consolidating Key Points

One of the reasons that "Engineering" isn't a subject area in most public schools is that it didn't exist as a domain when the modern school was invented. (The same can be said of "Technology.") What's your thinking on the matter? Should it be included as a separate subject area?

It might be useful, in formulating and defending your opinion, to do some research on some of the many great innovations that started in basements and garages. For example, motivated to provide affordable gasoline-powered vehicles, Henry Ford built the first quadricycle in his home and tested it in 1896. Spurred by a desire to offer people personal computers with intuitive interfaces, Steve Jobs, Steve Wozniak, and Ronald Wayne created the first Apple computers in the late 1970s. Similar themes appear in the histories of other multinationals, such as Microsoft, Samsung, Google, Facebook, and Netflix – to name a few.

Did these companies emerge *because of* schooling, or *in spite of* schooling?

Summing up

Where do the most disruptive innovations happen?

It would seem reasonable to imagine that the hotbeds of transformative thinking and creative engineering would be the places with the most resources, such as multinational corporations, research universities, and major government agencies. After all, not only are these organizations equipped to support new thinking, they are explicitly defined by their efforts toward and responsibilities for innovation.

And they certainly are sites of important engineering feats. However, it's not very hard to generate lists of innovative engineering accomplishments that happened in basements, dorm rooms, garages, and coffee shops. The bottom line is that, if large organizations were truly the main hotbeds of innovation, then it would be reasonable to expect that the first big company out of the blocks with a new product would be able to retain its advantage, staying ahead of possible competitors by pumping its greater profits into research and development.

But while successful companies attempt to stay ahead by doing exactly that, a surprising portion of innovation continues to happen outside of corporate settings. With that point in mind, the main reason for the growing emphasis on engineering education in public schools is not to provide industry with a larger workforce. Rather, it is to support attitudes, dispositions, and skill sets that are useful for everyone – and, in the process, to present youth with a nuanced understanding of engineering as a possible career path.

How and when did Nicole parse the learning goals? How did Nicole monitor students' understandings? What might have gone awry in the classroom during this exploration? How might Nicole have modified her teaching in response to student and classroom needs? How did Nicole keep the connections to the learning goals and the engineering design processes in balance?

Innovating Challenges

When we teach classes in STEM Education, our assignments typically revolve around creating engineering tasks (similar to the catapult activity) for different grade levels. Unfortunately, when we describe these assignments to course participants, many leap to the conclusion that we're asking them to invent their own tasks.

This is huge a misconception. Designing learning environments rarely involves starting from scratch. Rather, developing quality STEM resources requires input from both teaching and STEM professions alike, and it requires more time than most classroom teachers have. Concisely, it's more about innovation than invention. Inventing tasks from scratch is almost always poor practice.

The tasks below are developed with that point in mind.

1. This task is based on the assumption that you've worked your way through the margin notes in this chapter. Those notes ask you to apply a model of iterative engineering processes to analyze the catapult activity that was introduced in this chapter's opening anecdote. The focus shifts a little for this task. Rather than use the model to analyze a completed activity, you're invited to use the model to adapt the design of a proposed activity.

   Do an internet search for "engineering design competitions." (We suggested you do this for different reasons in the "Consolidating Key Ideas" box on p. 80.) Select a competition challenge that you find engaging, provocative, and/or compelling. Revisit the Asking–Imagining–Planning–Creating–Testing–Improving margin notes, considering the issues raised in those notes in relation to the task you've chosen.

2. There are many (perhaps too many) teaching resources on the internet. Being able to discern among online offerings and to select appropriate resources is a very important teaching skill.

   But how do you know if a resource is "good"? Even resources from reputable publishers and prominent government agencies can be recipe-like, constrain exploration, and limit thinking. What should you look for?

   To help you in this direction, we recommend the following sites as good starting places for resources:

   - Alternative Learning Place (mainly elementary level)
     http://www.alternativelearningplace.com/engineering6-9.cfm
   - Teaching Engineering Editor's Picks (elementary and secondary levels)
     https://www.teachengineering.org/view_activity.php?url=collection/cub_/activities/cub_human/cub_human_lesson06_activity3.xml
   - NASA's Best Activity Guides (elementary and secondary levels)
     http://www.nasa.gov/audience/foreducators/best/activities.html#.Vt28vccg3UA
   - stemNRICH (elementary and secondary levels)
     https://nrich.maths.org/stemnrich
   - Royal Academy of Engineers (elementary and secondary levels)
     https://www.tes.com/member/RoyalAcademyofEngineering

   Have a browse and pick a task from any of these sites.

   Revisit Figure 5.2 and the surrounding discussion. We identified three key elements of processes associated with innovation, namely thinking, playing, and building. Analyze your chosen tasks for these elements. Sample questions you might ask include:

- **THINKING** – Does the task compel students to think about the scientific principles involved? What sorts of demands does it place on the learner? Can the task be completed by anyone, or is there a specialized knowledge (e.g., of levers) that might be applied and developed within the task?

- **PLAYING** – Is there flexibility in the task, or is it overly prescriptive and/or recipe-like? Are participants compelled to explore and experiment, or is the task more about following steps?

- **BUILDING** – How much creativity is needed for the task? Is it a matter of gathering and assembling prefabricated parts, or are participants required to design, manufacture, and/or hone pieces? How much "ownership" might students take in the task? Will they see themselves as following instructions or as active inquirers?

You might have noticed that there's a good deal of overlap among these three categories. There's a good reason for that. They're all focused on different aspects of innovation. A task that is truly reflective of the field of engineering should compel innovative thinking, innovative playing, and innovative building.

Chapter 6

Science

method   inquiring

IN BRIEF

Science **education** has tended to focus on facts and methods, in contrast to research scientists' focuses on fact-connecting theories and the inquiries that support those theories.

Schooling is often focused on the **learning** of individuals. But collectives also learn. Scientific inquiry provides a window into knowledge-producing processes on both levels.

Teaching is about designing learning environments so students can become designers of scientific inquiry, able to pose questions and seek answers that matter to them and the world.

Inquiring Challenges   VIDEO LINK: https://vimeo.com/135752168

In their Decomposition Lab, Amy and Deidre's Grade-4 students conducted an inquiry into how fruits and vegetables rot through a 2½-week period.

It's immediately obvious in the video clips from the event that the children were captivated by the decomposition of fruits and vegetables – which isn't surprising. The topic of rotting produce was relevant to their existences, was fitted to their background knowledge, and lent itself to the observation skills they had developed. But more importantly, for many, it had an appealing "gross" factor. As well, Amy and Deidre's guiding question, "What happens to a perishable fruit/ veggie over a 2½-week period?", is very much along the lines of a question that expert researchers might pose for themselves. The topic is "elastic" that is, it can be stretched across wide ranges of age and expertise.

Notice how the children were not left to their own devices in planning and managing the investigation. Amy and Deidre were deliberate in their scaffolding of student work and they devoted considerable time and effort to ensuring

the children were prepared to conduct the investigation scientifically. For example, their first step was to have a brainstorming session with the children to generate the questions that would guide inquiry and focus observations. Specific topics investigated by different students included impact of temperature on rot, relationship to light and mold growth, effects of sealing items in jars and bags, among others.

On the surface, that brainstorming activity might appear as the "State the Problem" step of the classical scientific method. It was more than that, though. By working with the children to generate answerable questions, Amy and Deidre were tapping into prior knowledge, helping learners distinguish between manageable and unmanageable questions, drawing on past experiences to identify variables that could contribute to decomposition, and so on. It was hardly a simple matter of posing an orienting question.

To help the children understand the standards associated with scientific work, a follow-up class discussion led to the development of an assessment rubric based on five criteria: inquiry, knowledge and skills, enhancing and supporting community, communication, and work habits. Children helped to specify the descriptors of each level of performance. The process not only supported students' understandings of expectations, it contributed to senses of ownership of both the inquiry and the assessment. Used formatively throughout the investigation, the rubric helped focus the children's efforts and allowed them to monitor their own progress.

Next, Amy and Deidre helped the children hone the inquiry by refining the problem(s), identifying the variables associated with the problem, and listing the materials needed to conduct the experiment. They provided a worksheet to help the children record their problems, hypotheses, questions, and observations. These preparations helped children understand what was needed to complete their investigations in the laboratory. Among the tools and procedures discussed, it was agreed digital instruments for measuring temperature and weight, cameras for tracking decomposition and documenting other observations, and Google spreadsheet for recording, analyzing, and sharing data.

Once in the lab, the children selected their preferred fruit and began their explorations. The appearances of maggots and fruit flies, along with the emergence of disgusting smells generated excitement among the children. Amy and Deidre helped to channel that excitement into systematic observations and records.

As spreadsheets began to be populated with data, Amy and Deidre made them public by linking them to the class's webpage. Parents were invited to supplement the teachers' feedback on the spreadsheets. An expert (i.e., a Grade-7 teacher with more advanced knowledge of the biology and decomposition) was invited to the class to provide more information, field questions, help interpret observations, and assist students in further refining their hypotheses.

As understandings emerged and abilities to articulate insights developed, students shared their knowledge publically through blogs and podcasts, providing further evidence of their understandings of the phenomenon of decomposition and the iterative process of scientific research – an engagement through which they recognized that *inquiry* was much more than applying a *method*.

Consolidating Key Points

What sort of a fact is a "scientific fact"?

There's a popular belief that to be a scientific fact, a notion must be generated or demonstrated through an experiment – but that's not necessarily the case. There are actually many types of scientific facts, and each is associated with a specific sort of method. Think about some of the things you know or have heard to be scientificially true. What made them facts? Our answer is in the next paragraph, so this might be a good place to pause to think about your answers to that question.

Four common modes of generating and validating scientific facts are:

- through natural observation and measurement. For example, the Linnaean classification system used in biology to organize living forms is based on extensive observations and comparisons;
- through experiment-based observation and measurement. For example, the chemical composition of water (combining hydrogen and oxygen) was determined through testing, demonstration, and replication;
- through theory, such as mathematical analysis. For example, in the early 1800s, based on Newton's theories, scientists proposed gravity could bend light; in the early 1900s, based on his general theory of relativity, Einstein calculated the amount of bending; but it was not until 1979 that this "gravitational lensing" was demonstrated through measurement of natural events;
- through definition, as agreed by members of scientific domains. For example, Pluto was once a planet, but it lost its status when the International Astronomical Union changed the definition of the word *planet*.

To complicate matters, it is rare that any one of these modes would operate exclusively. Most often multiple aspects are at play in a scientific inquiry.

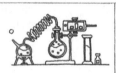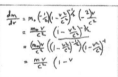

Another major influence on popular beliefs about scientific truth is the metaphor, "knowledge as object" – which, as developed in Chapter 2, is perhaps the most prominent metaphor of knowledge in everyday English. Modern science actually bolstered it with the metaphor of "objectivity," which was intended to collect notions such as stability, replicability, generalizability, and context independence. But the metaphor came with unwanted baggage. For example, it might be taken to suggest that there's such a thing as an observerless observation.

Revisit the tables used to analyze metaphors for knowledge and learning in Chapter 2. As you read through this chapter, think about which clusters are best fitted to scientific inquiry.

STEM Education

For many, "science" is understood mainly in terms of what they encountered in grade school classrooms. For that reason, the domain of science is often seen to comprise a collection of assertions that are supported by evidence and a standardized set of procedures to generate that evidence.

More explicitly, in the context of schooling, the word *science* is typically heard to refer to the pairing of two perceived-to-be-distinct aspects:

Knowledge Building Principle:

COMMUNITY KNOWLEDGE, COLLECTIVE RESPONSIBILITY

- scientific *facts* – that is, a static collection of established observations, principles, and laws on what the universe is and how it works;
- scientific *method* – that is, a rigorous strategy of experimentation, observation, and verification that's used to validate scientific facts.

Participants collaborate on a product demonstrating individual or collective learning.

Among research scientists, in contrast, these categories are seen as complementary, inseparable, and co-evolving. By way of visual metaphor, they might be represented as two dynamically interconnected aspects of the same whole. (See Figure 6.1.) An implication is that facts prompt questions, which are investigated with methods, which generate new or compel revision of facts, which prompt new questions, and so on.

There were many ways that Amy and Deidre provided opportunities for developing collective responsibility for advancing knowledge. What are a few of those? What preparations were likely necessary? What strategies did Amy and Deidre employ?

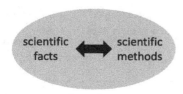

Figure 6.1. A visual metaphor for mutually dependent scientific facts and scientific methods

In school science, the dynamic interplay of facts and methods doesn't always come through so clearly. Facts are often presented as pregiven and fixed; methods are often recipe-like prescriptions. But the ideas of evolving-fact-influencing methods and evolving-method-influencing facts are not always foregrounded

Knowledge Building Principle:

CONSTRUCTIVE USE OF AUTHORITATIVE SOURCES

Participants critically evaluate information sources.

As children articulated their hypotheses and recorded their observations, Amy and Deidre challenged them to be aware of the roots of their interpretations and observations. What sorts of questions did they ask? What sorts of authoritative sources might they have used?

– which, in turn, might give the false impression that science is a closed and finished domain. Curriculum guides and classroom resources are typically focused on truths to be memorized, laws to be applied, and procedures to be mastered through routine, recipe-like repetitions of classic experiments. For example, a common one in the middle years revolves around determining which features of a simple pendulum affect how quickly it swings. Typically, students are tasked with systematically varying and testing such elements as the mass of the bob, the length of the string, the height of the drop, and the force of a push. Through rigorous application of method, they are expected to conclude that the only important factor in the period of a simple pendulum is the length of its string. The step-by-step "experiment" leads to an unimpeachable truth.

Before going further, we want to be clear that we don't mean to diminish the importance of the coupling of facts and methods in science. As this chapter's anecdote illustrates, these two elements are integral to inquiry. To prepare for and situate the experiment, the teachers skillfully summoned and introduced relevant established facts. That set the stage for posing appropriate problems, offering reasonably informed hypotheses, and designing manageable scientific studies. But did it stop there? Is scientific inquiry the sum of facts and methods?

Our (probably obvious) answers to each of these questions is, "No." Those two aspects do not come close to covering the range of activities entailed by the word *science*. In particular, they obscure the place and nature of *scientific theory* and they oversimplify some of the complexities of *scientific inquiry*. As explored in this chapter, a scientific theory is more than a collection of scientific facts, and a scientific inquiry is more than application of scientific methods. Many examples could be cited to illustrate these points. To this end, we use the "Consolidating Key Points" boxes in this chapter to take a closer look at some scientific facts and theories, and we use the margin notes to unpack some key qualities of scientific methods and inquiry.

To be clear, the examples presented in the margins are not intended to diminish the role of facts and methods in science. Rather, the point is to situate facts and methods in the grander cultural enterprise of science. Scientific study is utterly reliant on established insights and systematic strategies, but it cannot be reduced to just facts and a rigid *method*. As we develop in this chapter – and as we believe is illustrated in the opening anecdote – science is a mode of *inquiring* in pursuit of powerful, explanatory theories.

Consolidating Key Points

Several years ago, *The Guardian* listed the following as among the current "big questions in science." [from: https://www.theguardian.com/science/2013/sep/01/20-big-questions-in-science]

- What is the universe made of?
- How did life begin?
- Are we alone in the universe?
- What makes us human?
- Why do we dream?
- Are there other universes?
- Where do we put all the carbon?
- How do we beat bacteria?
- Will we ever cure cancer?
- What's at the bottom of the ocean?
- What's at the bottom of a black hole?
- How do we ensure humanity survives and flourishes?

Linking back to the previous "Consolidating Key Points" box, what sorts of scientific methods are likely to be used in each of these cases. Which questions would involve more than one type of fact (and more than one type of method)?

What is "science education"?

One way to understand a cultural phenomenon is to look at its controversies. What are its sticking points? Where do arguments arise and where are criticisms focused? What gets people fussed?

For science education, perhaps the biggest point of contention is the topic of evolutionary theory. Scorned and derided by some, and defended with passion by others, the theory of evolution is a hot-button issue that is often identified as a key marker in the failure of school science. One extreme identifies it as a failure because "it's only a theory" among many theories; another sees it as a failure because "it's not just a theory."

Which is it?

Neither, really.

At issue in these debates is that everyday uses of the word theory and its meaning in the phrase "scientific theory" are not compatible. In everyday terms, a theory is an interpretation that is useful for making sense of things, and often it doesn't much matter if that theory has inconsistencies, or if there are instances it can't explain, or if it contains contradictions, or if there is evidence to dispute it. For example, many young children have theorized that the sun and the moon are about the same size. Or every time a teacher designs a lesson, it's based on a personal theory that it will support students' learning.

A *scientific theory* is something entirely different. It is not an opinion; it cannot contain contradictions or inconsistencies; it must be accountable to all available evidence. That is, whereas an "everyday theory" is typically context-dependent and experience-based, a "scientific theory" is a more encompassing form of knowledge that applies across contexts and experiences. A scientific theory must be able to account for every observation. This requirement to be accountable to all observations means that scientific theories are always subject to revision or even outright rejection – which is a strength, not a weakness. Science proceeds on the assumption that all ideas are improvable; there is no perfect, finished knowledge awaiting discovery.

That is, scientific theories evolve. They are caught up in ecosystems of ideas and events that compel them to adapt if they are going to survive. On this count, a particularly vital aspect in the development of scientific theories is the presence of conflicting interpretations. In science, arguments and debates are vital aspects of the work, not things to be avoided. Disagreements may sometimes be seen and experienced as oppositions, but at the level of knowledge production they are actually opportunities. Occasions in which competing sets of observations and facts can be explained in more than one way invite further inquiry – additional

Knowledge Building Principle:

EMBEDDED AND TRANSFORMATIVE ASSESSMENT

Externally defined assessment is taken seriously but does not dominate knowledge work.

Besides a rubric, Amy and Deidre provided many other forms of embedded assessment to deepen student understanding. What were some of those? When did they occur? Were there opportunities for peers or people outside the classroom to provide feedback as well?

explorations, gathering more data, generating further hypotheses. That means that scientific inquiry isn't a linear trajectory toward a perfected knowledge of the universe; it is an ongoing, ever-branching conversation that must defend each of its assertions.

Returning to contemporary school-based debates about evolution, then, the "theory of evolution" is a scientific theory. It is a robust-but-always-subject-to-revision explanation that reaches across a broad range of observations and that has always been responsive to new evidence. Hence the populist critique that evolution – or any other scientific theory – is "just a theory" demonstrates a debilitatingly ignorant attitude toward the project of modern science.

Therein lies one of the major challenges of contemporary school science. How might the subject be formatted to nudge learners toward an appreciation of the true power and complexity of the scientific enterprise?

Our belief is that a response must begin with an appropriate model of the relationships among the notions of scientific fact, scientific method, scientific theory, and scientific inquiry. One way to model these associations is illustrated in Figure 6.2.

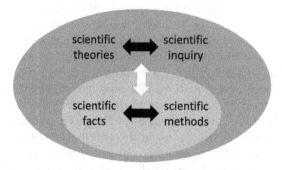

Figure 6.2. A visual metaphor relating among scientific facts-and-methods and scientific theories-and-inquiry

As emphasized in the previous section, school science has historically focused on the inner region of this diagram – on the interplay of facts and method. In contrast, many current efforts toward the reform of school science recommend increased attention on

Knowledge Building Principle:
DEMOCRATIZING KNOWLEDGE

Everyone's work is recognized; participants help each other find needed information.

Ensuring that each individual is contributing and being heard requires having strategies. How did Amy and Deidre ensure that each child was contributing to the data collection?

Knowledge Building Principle:
EPISTEMIC AGENCY

Participants demonstrate personal senses of direction, power, motivation, and responsibility

How did students represent their ideas? How did they negotiate a fit to personal ideas and the ideas of others? How did students develop autonomy in the inquiry?

Knowledge Building Principle:

IDEA DIVERSITY

Different ideas or opinions are brainstormed, clustered, and debated to generate new insight.

At the start of the inquiry, Amy and Deidre brainstormed ideas with the class. What were those ideas? How did those ideas fit with and contribute to the unfolding scientific inquiry?

Knowledge Building Principle:

IMPROVABLE IDEAS

Ideas are accepted or rejected on the basis of logical argument and evidence

How did the children collect data? How did they verify accuracy? What tools did they use? How did they record their data? How did they analyse and present/report their findings?

the outer level. With this contrast in mind, it's worth pausing for a moment to reflect on the origins of the entrenched emphasis on the facts–methods level – and, in particular, to interrogate specific and narrow interpretations of the "scientific method" that are most often associated with that level. What is it? Where did it come from? And why is it nearly ubiquitous in curricula and resources developed for school science?

While there are many variations among descriptions and definitions of the scientific method in educational materials, there are some strong themes across most suggestions. A quick internet search of "scientific method" will confirm that most descriptions are structured around a sequence that is similar to the following:

- **PROBLEM POSING** – Ask a question.

- **HYPOTHESIS FORMULATING** – Learn as much as possible about what's already known of the problem, and use that knowledge to make an educated conjecture.

- **METHOD DESIGNING** – Design a procedure that will make it possible to test your hypothesis systematically.

- **DATA GATHERING** – Perform the experiment, taking care to record data clearly and systematically.

- **DATA ANALYZING** – Use appropriate methods to identify and characterize patterns in the data.

- **INFERENCE DRAWING** – Make and report inferences based on the analyzed data.

With regard to common variations on this sequence, descriptions sometimes include steps to revise or refine the problem, to retest or verify results, to subject results to the scrutiny of other scientists, and to link to other results with a view toward the formulation of a theory.

One of the frequent critiques of such versions of the scientific method is that they might give the impression that doing science is mainly a linear, "cookbook" process. It isn't, of course. However, such representations are correct on a few points. The tidy, linear format underscores the importance of clear thinking, systematic analysis, coherent argument, and replicability. That said, linearized versions can obscure the actual messiness of scientific inquiry – of blind alleys, inexplicable results, contradictory conclusions, and such.

The reason for the difference between the idealized scientific method and the actual branching complexity of most scientific inquiry is informative. It turns out that the linear conception of the scientific method is an invention of educators who derived it from the structure of scientific reporting (Rudolph, 2005) – that is, not from actual scientific inquiries, but from summaries of inquiries in which writers deliberately stripped down the details to tell about completed and successful experiments. It makes sense that such reports would ignore blind alleys and unsuccessful efforts, focusing instead on the things that worked in a tightly scripted problem–hypothesis–method–results–inference sequence. In other words, the version of the scientific method that has become so prominent in the educational literature is actually a fiction – it is a reflection of the way results are usually reported, not a description of the way that research is typically envisioned and undertaken.

Consequently, the familiar, linearized scientific method so often found in the educational literature obscures some vital elements of scientific inquiry. For example, in practice scientists engage in a broader range of activities – and do so in different orders, as fitted to their expertise, emerging issues and possibilities, and many other circumstances. Collectively these instances show that scientific knowledge is more than a compilation of facts generated by researchers. Rather, it is a vibrant, evolving, theory-oriented enterprise that emerges in the interactions of people, their ideas, and the more-than-human world.

For these reasons, current models of the workings of science – such as the one we offer on the next page – tend to employ circular or cyclical forms, highlighting that science is never complete and always situated. The reporting and replicating of new insights present the possibilities of new or reformulated questions; the application of new knowledge helps to shape the world, which in turn shapes the questions asked. We offer our own simplified model for the nested and endlessly recursive processes of science in Figure 6.3.

Knowledge Building Principle:

PERVASIVE KNOWLEDGE BUILDING

Time is set aside for creative work with ideas; special supports encourage creative work.

Where and how was creativity encouraged and expected? (It might be useful to think in terms of the steps commonly associated with the scientific method (as listed on page 97) and to contrast such characterizations with the complexified model of inquiry (presented on p. 99).

Another more richly nuanced model has been created by a consortium at the University of California Berkeley as part of their "Understanding Science: how science really works" interactive website (http://undsci. berkeley.edu/). We urge you to vist the site and explore the layers, the embeddings, and the sequences they use to illustrate and animate the project of modern science. While it is quite different from what we offer in Figure 6.3, both models are focused on the interplay of facts and methods. And both highlight that the project of scientific inquiry is much larger than is typically represented in schools.

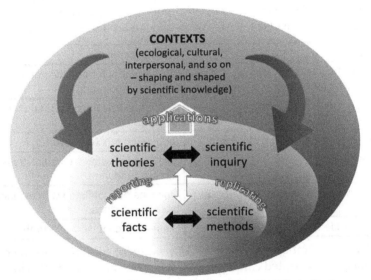

Figure 6.3. One model of the complex cultural project of science

This sort of nested, nonlinear model does a better job of foregrounding some of the exciting, dynamic, unpredictable, and surprising aspects of scientific inquiry, as well as situating science as a historical, social, and cultural enterprise (Zemplén, 2009). Not only does it paint a different picture of what science is all about, it illustrates the inadequacy of the word *method* to capture what it means to do science. It was precisely this sort of thinking that prompted educators over the last several decades to move to the notion of *inquiry*.

Consolidating Key Points

Every year, the *Oxford English Dictionary* selects a "word of the year" – a term that the editors feel is reflective of important developments or trends. In 2016, their choice was "post-truth," which they defined on their website as "relating to or denoting circumstances in which objective facts are less influential in shaping public opinion than appeals to emotion and personal belief."

The choice would appear to be a good one. It was a year in which the science of climate change, evolution, immunization, and other established knowledge was openly and unabashedly criticized … and even publicly scorned. Personal beliefs were regularly placed on par with objective facts.

How does the teacher of science fit into this post-truth era?

Our answer is that the teacher is responsible for representing the domain, and so must have robust understandings of the differences between objective fact and subjective opinion, between science and pseudoscience, between *scientific* and *scientistic*, and so on. Consider the following table (adapted from Coker, 2001).

Science	Pseudoscience
Rigorous standards for honesty and accuracy, including a peer review process.	No standards for or expectations of accuracy and precision.
All results must be replicable.	Some results can't be reproduced or verified.
Examines and learns from failures.	Ignores or conceals failures.
Knowledge is emergent.	Knowledge is static. Original ideas are rarely abandoned.
Must answer to all available evidence.	Opinions are conflated with evidence-based assertions.
Biases are identified, when possible.	Biases are confused with truth.

There are some important parallels between these columns and the clusters of learning theories presented earlier. Revisit the seven summary tables in Chapter 2. Is the science–pseudoscience contrast useful for categorizing theories of learning?

Now consider these topics: extrasensory perception, climate change, detoxes and vitamin therapies, evolution, intelligent design. In which category – i.e., science or pseudoscience – does each belong? (Note that there is a correct answer in each case. If you have trouble categorizing one, you might want to delve more deeply.)

Now watch ecologist Suzanne Simard's TED Talk, "How trees talk to each other" [https://www.ted.com/talks/suzanne_simard_how_trees_talk_to_each_other]. She discusses how trees communicate, often over great distances. Her phrasing is deliberately provocative. It's intended to compel hearers to consider the possibility that trees have complicated social lives and that there is much more to forests than is typically imagined … but she has been criticized for overstating or mischaracterizing the case. Is she doing science? Is it pseudoscience?

What is "inquiry"?

Inquiry is about the iterative process of working with established facts and accumulating additional evidence in order to defend, extend, and/or challenge interpretations. That means that inquiry is a complex notion that involves the integration of several facets of knowledge. We'll focus on two here: knowledge building and disciplinary expertise.

Knowledge building and inquiry

Knowledge Building Principle:

REAL IDEAS, AUTHENTIC PROBLEMS

Project-based learning replaces short-term tasks with more complex, ill-defined tasks.

Amy and Deidre's choice of task around understanding how fruits and vegetables rot definitely piqued their students' interest. However, it was the choice and sequencing of sub-tasks that helped them understand their world. What were some of the sub-tasks that helped students gain this understanding? How did all the sub-tasks deepen and advance new knowledge?

Every academic domain is associated with inquiry, although not all modes of academic inquiry can be properly called "scientific." Before we dig into what sets scientific inquiry apart, let us first review some of the elements of inquiry that are common across all domains.

Scardamalia and Bereiter (2014) have spent decades looking into "knowledge building" – that is, necessary conditions and powerful practices that enable a community to develop knowledge. Table 6.1 (on pp. 102–103) provides a summary of their model. As well, we have used them in this chapter's margin notes to highlight and interpret aspects of the opening anecdote.

A first detail to notice is that many of the principles named in the left column are consistent with the descriptions of science that have been discussed and the models that have been illustrated in previous sections of this chapter. .

While it would be inappropriate to suggest that enacting Scardamalia and Bereiter's principles of knowledge building are synonymous with inquiry, the model offers a powerful starting place for teachers who wish to sponsor inquiries in their classrooms, regardless of subject matter. Regarding STEM domains, and as we have emphasized repeatedly in every chapter, there's a big difference between "knowing the facts" and really understanding how knowledge from mathematics, technology, engineering, and science live in the world. For the latter, students need to take part in the collective process of creating insight – that is, of "knowledge building."

Table 6.1. Elements of Scardamalia and Bereiter's (2006) Knowledge Building

Principle	Standard Best Practice	Knowledge Building Value Added
Community Knowledge, Collective Responsibility	Participants collaborate on the production of a finished product that demonstrates individual or small-group learning.	Participants take responsibility for the overall advancement of knowledge in the community.
Constructive Uses of Authoritative Sources	Participants critically evaluate information sources and recognize that even the best are fallible.	Participants use authoritative sources, along with other information sources as data for their own processes of building knowledge and improving ideas.
Embedded and Transformative Assessment	Externally defined assessment is taken seriously but does not dominate knowledge work.	The community engages in its own internal assessment, which is both more fine-tuned and rigorous than external assessment, and serves to ensure that the community's work will exceed the expectations of external assessors.
Democratizing Knowledge	Everyone's work is recognized and praised; participants help each other find needed information.	All participants are legitimate contributors to the shared goals of the community; all have a sense of ownership of knowledge advances achieved by the group.
Epistemic Agency	Participants demonstrate a personal sense of direction, power, motivation, and responsibility.	Participants mobilize personal strengths to set forth their ideas and to negotiate a fit between personal ideas and ideas of others, using contrasts to spark and sustain knowledge advancement rather than depending on others to chart that course for them.
Idea Diversity	Different ideas or opinions are brainstormed, and then grouped into categories, and finally arguments are carried out to resolve differences.	Different ideas create a dynamic environment in which contrasts, competition, and complementarity of ideas is evident, creating a rich environment for ideas to evolve into new and more refined forms.
Improvable Ideas	Ideas are accepted or rejected on the basis of logical argument and evidence.	All ideas are treated as improvable; participants aim to mirror the work of great thinkers in gathering and weighing evidence, and ensuring that explanations cohere with all available evidence.

Pervasive Knowledge Building	Special time is set aside for creative work with ideas, usually after the basic work is done; special technologies and supports encourage work.	Creative work with ideas is integral to all knowledge work.
Real Ideas, Authentic Problems	Project-based learning replaces short-term tasks with more complex, ill-defined tasks.	Real knowledge problems arise from efforts to understand the world; creative work with ideas supports faster and more reliable learning, whereas learning alone seldom leads to knowledge innovation.
Rise Above	Leader takes responsibility for synthesizing diverse ideas, identifying common ground, and presenting new challenges.	The conditions to which people adapt change as a result of the successes of other people in the environment. Adapting means adapting to a progressive set of conditions that keep raising standards.
Knowledge Building Discourse	Discourse allows participants to express and gain feedback on their ideas, defend different points of view, arrive at conclusions.	Discourse serves to identify shared problems and gaps in understanding and to advance understanding beyond the level of the most knowledgeable individual.
Symmetric Knowledge Advancement	Groups carry out inquiries independently and then publicize their findings for the benefit and response of other groups.	Interleaved communities provide successively more demanding contexts for knowledge work, and set into motion inner-outer community dynamics that serve to embed ideas.

Disciplinary knowledge within scientific inquiry

What distinguishes *scientific inquiry* from *inquiry*?

As is evident in Table 6.1, knowledge building involves a continual process of sharing and improving on what is already known. Experts in a field of study are always pushing these boundaries, leading to new insights that can change lives. This spirit of inquiry can also take place in schools where students are willing and capable to take on the challenges of the outside world. As students develop knowledge-building competencies, they come to see themselves and their work as part of the effort to advance the frontiers of what we know as a society, and indeed contribute in a meaningful way to the body of work within a discipline.

All those elements are necessary to scientific inquiry. However, they aren't sufficient for an inquiry to be scientific. For that, attention must be given to the specific demands of each branch of science. Each discipline constitutes a distinctive way of thinking about some category of phenomena; each entails a mode of engagement that is modeled by skilled scientists responsible for advancing knowledge within the discipline. A first step in describing scientific inquiry is thus to acknowledge the range of scientific domains. Table 6.2 offers a partial picture.

Many categories and schemes have been devised to distinguish among types of science – a point that can be easily demonstrated through internet searches of "types" or "categories" or "branches" of sciences. Each of these domains has its own methods of inquiry – since, for example, phenomena as diverse as the fossil record and lightning don't lend themselves to the

Table 6.2. Some branches, sub-branches, and hybrid branches of contemporary science

	Physical sciences	Life sciences	Earth sciences	
Leaning toward experiment-based trials and evidence	Physics Kinetics Mechanics Electromagnetics Thermodynamics	Biology Botany Ecology Zoology	Geology Meteorology Astronomy Oceanography	Leaning toward naturalistic observations and measurements
	Chemistry Inorganic Chemistry Electrochemistry Analytical Chemistry			
	Examples of Hybrid Sciences			
	Physics + Chemistry = Physical Chemistry Astronomy + Physics = Astrophysics	Biology + Chemistry = Biochemistry Organic Chemistry Biology + Geology = Paleontology Biology + Astronomy + Physics = Astronautics	Geology + Chemistry = Geochemistry Geology + Astronomy = Astrogeology	

same strategies of observation. However, that doesn't mean the methods are entirely distinct. What is common to all are such qualities as rigorous standards of observation, verification, and replicability, as well as an uncompromising expectation that current scientific theories must account for all current scientific facts.

Once again, it is this quality that distinguishes scientific knowledge from other domains of human knowing. Science must be responsible to the world. While it is possible for there to be more than one scientific theory to account for the same set of facts, a scientific theory cannot persist in the face of contradictory facts. That's not the case with non-scientific theories, pseudoscience, and popular worldviews. Consider, for example, conflicting religious sensibilities or opposing political ideologies. In these cases, there is no obligation to attend to empirical evidence. Inquiries oriented by specific belief systems or ideologies can (and often do) ignore or cherry-pick evidence, even while enacting the principles of knowledge building.

On its own, knowledge building offers a great deal of useful advice to science teachers. However, knowledge building is just one of the "Task Design Principles" introduced in Chapter 4, and it should be considered alongside others when making the transition from the cultural project of "scientific inquiry" to the educational project of "science class." They're not the same thing and shouldn't be conflated.

With that point in mind, consider how each of the Task Design Principles from Chapter 4 was addressed in the inquiry into decomposition:

- **COMMON GOAL** – All learners examined the process of decomposition over a period of time.
- **MULTIPLE SOLUTIONS** – The inquiry spanned a range of factors that can contribute to decomposition, including temperature, humidity, light, mould, and airflow. Each group of students investigated a specific variable on a specific fruit, all of their choosing, thus contributing to broader understandings of the phenomena when findings were pooled.
- **VARIABLE ENTRY** – Supported through well-structured discussion and other scaffolds, children

Knowledge Building Principle:

RISE ABOVE

Leader takes responsibility for synthesizing ideas and presenting new challenges.

What strategies did (or might have) Amy and Deidre utilize to capitalize on the success of individuals and small groups to support and advance the understandings of the collective group?

were able to translate their initial interests and background knowledge into answerable questions.

- **PURPOSEFUL PRACTICE** – Elements of the scientific method, such as measuring, observing, and recording data, were engaged in critically reflective manners that alerted learners to the importance of tools and techniques that are well fitted to the phenomenon under investigation.

- **TASK FEEDBACK** – Google spreadsheets enabled teachers and parents to comment and to ask questions, thus providing timely formative feedback.

- **SOFT SKILLS** – All aspects of the inquiry were highly interactive, and many required negotiation and collaboration. That is, the inquiry was a site to learn and practice a range of interpersonal skills that are useful in and beyond scientific work.

- **LEARNING TRANSFER** – The inquiry drew on and reinforced learnings from mathematics and language arts classes. For instance, students were routinely required to use decimal fractions to make measurements and calculations, and their daily observations were expected to be well articulated.

- **KNOWLEDGE BUILDING** – By working together to examine different contributing factors of decomposition, individual and collective understandings of decomposition were deepened.

- **COMPETENCY-BASED ASSESSMENT** – Amy and Diedre had many benchmarks for assessing students' learning of decomposition, specifically, and scientific inquiry, generally. The Google spreadsheets were particularly useful in this regard, as they served as a site to collect measurements, calculations, observations, and interpretations. They were also highly adaptable, enabling Amy and Diedre to tweak elements on the fly as the inquiry unfolded.

- **PRIORITIZING LEARNING** – Each of the technologies for the scientific inquiry were carefully chosen for learning about decomposition. For instance, digital thermometers and balances were chosen because they were fitted to young learners' skills in reading scales and performing calculations.

Knowledge Building Principle:
KNOWLEDGE BUILDING DISCOURSE

Discourse enables feedback, defending points of view, and making new conclusions.

When students encountered difficulties or new insights, were there opportunities for them to share or discuss these issues? Who did they discuss them with? How might issues have been resolved?

At first glance, these Task Design Principles may seem like a checklist of items. It is perhaps more appropriate to think of them as nodes in an interlinked network. None can be completely dissociated from the others; each is more powerful when considered in relation to the others.

There is one other vital element to in-school inquiry that we haven't addressed yet: the mandated curriculum. With regard to the context of the decomposition inquiry, there are six core topics in the Grade 4 Alberta Education (1996) Science Program of Studies. The inquiry contributed to at least three of those topics: Waste and Our World; Light and Shadows; and, Plant Growth and Changes – in addition to addressing more generalized requirements associated with scientific inquiry in the Program of Study. We emphasize this point because, in our experience, discussions of "inquiry" in science class are often associated with trade-offs and tensions – for example, pitting student interest against curriculum coverage, or content against skills. As the episode demonstrated, it is entirely possible to avoid such issues in well-designed inquiries.

Consolidating Key Points

Barrow (1993) once noted, in reference to the development and acceptance of scientific theories, that "Arguments against new ideas generally pass through three distinct stages, from, 'It's not true,' to, 'Well, it may be true, but it's not important,' to, 'It's true and it's important, but it's not new – we knew it all along.'"

Barrow's characterization was intended to be "humorously accurate." Indeed, many theories that are now broadly accepted were initially greeted with more than skepticism, in both scientific and popular arenas. Some examples include non-geocentric models of the universe, Continental Drift (Plate Tectonics), Gaia Hypothesis, and Complexity Theory. Pick one or two of these theories (or add to the list, if you're aware of others) and do some research into their developments and the rocky roads to their eventual acceptance.

Familiarity with such details can be important for teaching. As Dweck (2007) has demonstrated, students who are exposed to the contentious histories are less likely to see science as a collection of facts to be memorized and procedures to be mastered, and more likely to see science as a domain of human engagement.

Summing up

School science is often experienced as the imposition of objective, depersonalized information – that is, about the opposite of engagement and design.

On some levels, that emphasis is justified. After all, the development of knowledge proceeds by drawing on and extending the insights of others. However, the project of understanding the universe more deeply would come to a grinding halt if everyone had to master every bit of established insight before tackling new questions.

The point of inquiry in the context of the school science classroom, then, isn't to rediscover or reconstruct every aspect of established scientific knowledge. It is to bring learners into the expansive, possibility-oriented, evidence-accountable attitude of science while, at the same time, afford opportunities to apply and master key skills and ideas that are likely of particular relevance to their existences.

No doubt that last sentence will sound heady and grandiose to some. But it shouldn't. As this chapter's opening anecdote illustrates, scientific inquiry can be designed in ways that make it relevant to almost any aspect of a child's existence. Much in contrast to the often-detached nature of the depersonalized facts and abstract formulas that students encounter in their science classes, an inquiry-based school science is about being more connected to one's world.

Knowledge Building Principle:

SYMMETRIC KNOWLEDGE ADVANCEMENT

Insights are communicated to support others' knowledge and to invite critical response.

How did students communicate their insights beyond the classroom? What strategies were used to import additional expertise into the classroom?

Inquiring Challenges

Designing scientific inquiry to engage students requires much more than following a prescribed method and memorizing facts. However, when we did a Google search to find examples of good, classroom-appropriate scientific inquiries, instead of encountering well-structured inquiries we were confronted with mostly craft-like and frequently scientifically dubious activities (e.g., "simulate an erupting volcano by using baking soda and vinegar") or experiments in which the questions and methods were already specified in rigid detail.

It's not difficult to figure out that such activities are unlikely to support scientific inquiry in the classroom. One need only examine them through the lenses of knowledge building, task design, and discipline-based inquiry. But, as important as it is to be able to sort out poor resources, more expertise is needed to select, adapt, and enact ideas to support scientific investigation.

Perhaps the most critical element in developing this expertise is the skill of translating students' interests and noticings into questions and methods that are appropriate to scientific research. The graphic below was designed with this concern in mind.

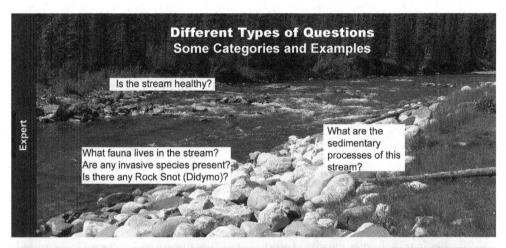

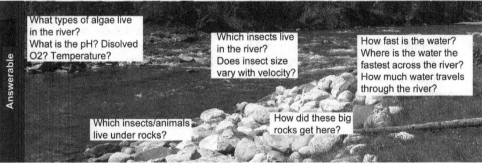

In the bottom panel of the graphic, we've listed some of the questions and observations that might be offered by elementary-aged children in the setting depicted. None of these articulations is expressed in a manner that supports a scientific inquiry, but each points to an interest that can move in that direction. To that end, in the top panel we've listed some questions that experts might ask.

1. What are some of the essential differences among the articulations in the bottom panel and the questions in the top? (To address this question, we recommend revisiting the margin notes, as well as the "What is 'inquiry'" section of this chapter, attending to both principles of knowledge building and specific qualities of scientific inquiry.)

2. Classroom-based inquiry should be oriented by children's interests, but it should never be reduced to simply pursuing their questions or observations. The teacher has an obligation to help them translate what they're noticing into questions that support scientific inquiry. Mindful of this detail, in the middle panel we've offered some "pedagogical translations" of the children's articulations.

    Do our translations reflect the "essential differences" between children's and experts' questions that you identified in response to Question 1? If not, how are they different? Would you offer different pedagogical translations of the children's articulations?

3. Earlier in this chapter we introduced a list of "big questions in science" assembled by *The Guardian*. Pick one and undertake an analysis similar to the one offered in the graphic on the preceding page. What might students ask or notice when presented with the question? (If you have access to students, you should consider asking them.) How might experts pose their questions? (We recognize this to be a difficult task that'll likely require research – which might include asking an expert – to answer.) Finally, how might you translate student articulations into questions that might orient a scientific inquiry?

Chapter 7

STEM Education

reception   contributing

IN BRIEF

Traditional STEM **education** has tended to focus on simplification and impartiality. This chapter looks at STEM education in terms of complexity and complicity.

Learners are often cast as passive recipients. More active, participatory and responsive descriptions – ones positioning learners as contributors rather than receptacles – are explored.

Teachers are not neutral conduits of knowledge. They are always active agents in shaping the world, and so there are ethical obligations to act mindfully as agents of change.

"Flood of the Century" hits a second time

CALGARY. In the first days of summer in 2013, a network of rivers in southern Alberta overflowed their banks. States of emergency were declared throughout the region, with several communities forced to evacuate homes and businesses. More than 100 000 people were displaced, and total damage exceeded $5 billion.

This disaster was the second "flood of the century" in less than a decade. Eight years previous, in 2005, $400 million in damages resulted when the two rivers that converge in the center of the city – the Bow and the Elbow – spilled over their banks. But much more water rushed through the city in 2013. At their peak, water levels were three times higher than they were in 2005, carrying roughly ten times more water than normal and flowing many times faster.

As with most natural disasters, there wasn't a singular cause to the 2013 flood. Calgary is located just east of the Rocky Mountains, and high water levels are typical in the late spring and early summer due to melting of mountain snow. Levels were slightly higher than normal in 2013, due largely to a heavy snow load from the previous winter, and that meant that the ground

was already quite saturated. Consequently, when an unusual weather pattern dropped 20–30 cm (8–12 inches) of rain across the region, not only did the massive downpour not soak in, it rapidly accelerated the melting of the snowpack.

Post-flood actions were swift. By November 2013, several projects had been announced to mitigate future flooding in the area, including construction of a channel to divert water and a dry dam upstream from major population centers. Funds were also directed toward feasibility studies of other proposals, such as tunnels and berms to divert flood waters away from neighborhoods and "improving" river banks so that they could better withstand massive floods.

Consolidating Key Points

As signalled by the opening anecdote/news story, this chapter's discussion is anchored to environmental events in which humans are complicit. If you weren't affected by that flood, you might consider other large-scale events (e.g., hurricanes, tornados, heatwaves, etc.) that might have affected you in some way. The discussion will likely be more relevant if you're able to refer to happenings in the first person (i.e., using "I" or "we") rather than the third person (i.e., using "he," "she," "xe," or "they") – that is, if you're able to look into a mirror rather than through a window.

STEM **E**ducation

While infrequent, large-scale environmental events such as the one described in this chapter's opening anecdote are becoming more commonplace, evidenced in the fact that two "floods of the century" were experienced eight years apart.

Our "report," above, is presented in the style and tone of a news story. In fact, its facts and figures were gleaned from a few dozen articles and we deliberately mimicked their structures, rhythms, and formats.

We did that to make a point. Or, rather, we did it to make several points. In particular, we wanted to highlight a relationship between this manner of impersonal, agentless report and the ends and emphases of traditional mathematics and science education. In the process, we wanted to set up a contrast with the intentions and possibilities of STEM Education as it is currently being envisioned. Our assertion, developed in this chapter, is that an impersonal and agentless report should be heard as odd and ill-fitting by a populace well schooled in STEM Education.

Consider some of the upshots of the sort of news report just presented. In our experience, the following reactions are common among friends, colleagues, and students:

In the margin notes in this chapter, we begin to parse some of the information that was pushed into the public realm after the 2013 Calgary flood. Our purpose is to use that flood as an illustrative example, providing entry ways into a range of possible STEM inquiries. We invite you to think about whether and how you might incorporate such information into your teaching of science, technology, engineering, and mathematics classes.

- **DE-COMPLEXIFICATION** and **DEFLECTION**: Listeners/readers tend to oversimplify as they look for singular causes – often, for example, invoking "climate change" as a unified, causal notion.

- **DESPAIR** and **DISTANCING**: Listeners/readers often express feelings of helplessness and hopelessness, and more because of the magnitude of the imagined cause than the actual event. For example, they often speak in the third person (e.g., "They need to do something") rather than the first person (e.g., "I/We must act") when discussing responses.

Might it be that such responses and reactions are related to an inadequate STEM Education? Might they be symptomatic of feelings of disenfranchisement that extend well beyond common responses to natural disasters and other major calamities, into all manner of large-scale events and developments that informed responses?

In other words, it is our belief that a well-structured STEM Education should occasion much different responses. Specifically, we feel that news of the sort reported above should trigger thoughts and feelings that are more toward the following:

In the summer of 2016, years after the flood, several rafts were punctured by partially submerged rebar in Calgary's Bow River. Multiple rescues were required.

The rebar had been deposited in 2013 by flood waters, highlighting that the event was still "current."

What sorts of inquiry questions arise for you here? How might those interests be formatted for classroom-based engagements?

- **APPRECIATION OF COMPLEXITY**: Listeners/readers don't attribute such events to singular causes, but rather consider constellations of contributing factors.

- **ATTUNEMENT TO COMPLICITY**: Listeners/readers feel implicated – that is, responsible and response-able, in some way. This is not to say that they take on a burden of blame, but that they recognize complicity, compelled to consider how their actions and desires might have contributed in some manner to the event. Listeners/readers feel enabled to act; they feel some level of agency, empowered to participate in responding to the event. While appropriate actions may not be immediately evident, listeners/readers are confident in their abilities to study the event and to insert themselves meaningfully.

For us, STEM Education is all about nurturing the understandings and dispositions that are necessary to trigger this cluster of responses. An effective STEM Education should do more than support learners' understandings of the complexities of their worlds; it should also support senses of agency and responsibility, and ideally it would culminate in feelings of being compelled and empowered to act. As learners and citizens, an effective STEM Education should disrupt their traditional roles as passive recipients of established knowledge and reposition them as active contributors with/in the more-than-human world.

Such ideals represent a dramatic departure from the aims of traditional mathematics and science education, which have at times seemed to be about disconnecting learners from their worlds and diminishing their agency. Underscoring this point, to our observation, among the many flood-focused news stories that also touched on the topic of schooling, not one was framed in terms of how the event might serve to orient inquiries or inform discussions. Rather, if and when formal education was mentioned, the concerns were about interruptions in exam schedules, damage to schools, needs to relocate students, and so on. In spite of the fact that the flood displaced 100 000 people, it didn't hit hard enough to nudge school mathematics and science out of their deeply carved ruts.

So how might schooling have responded differently?

This chapter is structured as one possible response to that question. We use the event as a case study of possibilities, aiming to illustrate how STEM Education might be conceived and enacted ... not as a new set of curriculum aims to be received, but as an entirely different way to think about what it means to educate and to be educated. A strong STEM Education doesn't merely position the learner as a *recipient*; it is more about *contributing* – that is, enacting a manner of knowing that cannot be separated from acting and being.

We proceed with a series of anecdotes, in which we offer a different way into talking about and reporting on the 2013 flood. (Some of the margin notes in this chapter offer additional anecdotal information.)

Calgary's landscape was carved by glaciation during the last ice age. As the glacier retreated Lake Calgary was left behind. The lake dried up around 12 000 years ago leaving escarpments, river basins that shaped the Bow River and the meltwater channels that evolved into the Elbow River system. Flooding is a natural part of the system, begging the question of why so many communities are built on flood plains.

Check out the Flood Hazard Map Application [http://maps.srd. alberta.ca/floodhazard/**].**

What is "STEM Education"?

"[E]ducation ... is a process of living and not a preparation for future living."

This assertion was made by John Dewey (1859–1952) in his 1897 publication, "My Pedagogic Creed." Dewey is regarded by many as the most influential North American educational thinker ... ever. The themes of "My Pedagogic Creed" still feel timely, pointing to both the progressive nature of Dewey's thinking and the sometimes-glacial pace of educational reform. (The full text is available at: http://dewey.pragmatism. org/creed.htm.)

We share Dewey's conviction that education is a process of living and we see this text as a reflection of his assertion. It is about formatting education in ways that make it integral to one's existence. It is as much about the past and the present as it is about the future.

Consolidating Key Points

With their usually cool, clear, mountain-fed waters, the Bow and Elbow Rivers are popular among sportfishers, many of whom predicted that fishing would be decimated after the flood.

They were correct. The fish larvae that had hatched just weeks earlier washed away in what biologists call a "year-class failure." For the provincially threatened westslope cutthroat trout, the loss was even more devastating. As the flood waters receded, more than 5000 fish – a fraction of the total that were stranded in pools beside the receding waters – were rescued by fisheries staff and volunteers. Fishing on the Elbow and Bow was closed for the rest of the season.

Yet, despite the devastation, flooding is part of the natural renewal of the river. The flood waters actually cleaned the gravel, washing out trapped sediment and making it easier for the next generation of fish larvae to survive. For the fall-spawning bull trout (a species of special concern), the cleaner gravel improved the chance of survival for hatchlings. The rushing water also created deep pools that help trout survive the winter.

- APPRECIATION OF COMPLEXITY: This story is focused on fish – as opposed to the many, many other species that were affected by the flood. What might be the reasons for this focus? What problems with interpretation might arise with a failure to consider the broader diversity of life in the river ecosystems?

- ATTUNEMENT TO COMPLICITY: This story prompted many "do-gooder" reactions, as people saw rescuing fish as a way to help. What issues might arise with this sort of focused "participation" (or, perhaps, "interference") in the ecosystem? What should be considered when making decisions in acting in such circumstances?

The set of anecdotes in the "Consolidating Key Points" sections of this chapter, as contrasted with the news-like report at the start of this chapter, is indicative of this conviction. Traditional mathematics and science education have focused on the presentation of facts, whereby the teacher delivers and the student receives. Those positionings align with a schooling that is only about preparation for adult life.

But a schooling that is about living is something entirely different, and it calls for additional ways of communicating the "facts" of mathematics and science. It is certainly the case that established, objectified truths must be presented, but there must also be footholds for subjective engagement. Lacking opportunities to situate information in their personal worlds, students will almost certainly be left to wonder "When are we going to use this?" and "Is this going to be on the test?" rather than appreciating that everything they are being asked to study is, in a very real way, about them.

We recommend reading the entirety of Dewey's four-page "Creed." For us, it resonates deeply with this chapter's core theme of regarding each student not just as a recipient of information, but as a contributor to knowledge. To develop this point more deeply, we use a few more of Dewey's provocations as the headers for the next two sections of this chapter.

The forest acts like a sponge during heavy rainfall, absorbing dramatically more water than can be absorbed by land stripped of trees. Clearcutting leaves the land barren and unable to hold water – thus increasing the risks of floods.

Industrial logging in areas upstream from Calgary, such as Kananaskis and Bragg Creek, likely contributed to the 2013 flood in Calgary. How might needs for wood products (for homes, paper, etc.) be balanced with flood mitigation?

"participation ... in the social consciousness"

"[A]ll education proceeds by the participation of the individual in the social consciousness of the race. ... [O]nly true education comes through the stimulation of the child's powers by the demands of the social situations in which he finds himself [sic]."

In academia, the "Arts and Humanities" are often separated from "Mathematics and Science." On one side of this divide sit those manners of expression and those modes of inquiry that are distinctly human. On the other side, it is commonly imagined, sit those domains that are committed to truths that are independent of our humanity – truths that will be truths long after the race perishes.

That's certainly the conception of mathematics and science that's represented in traditional schooling, and it helps to explain the entrenched emphases on disciplinarity, acquisition, computation, usage,

---

Consolidating Key Points

My family lives 11 blocks north of the Bow River. We felt the first major impact of the flood on our youngest daughter's birthday, when heavy rainfall prevented my parents and sisters from coming over for the celebratory dinner.

With the interruption of that event, we decided to walk to the river to check out the rising water. As we approached, our first observation was that the space between the water level and the 14th Street Bridge, normally more than adequate to accommodate a large vessel, likely wasn't enough to allow even our canoes to slip through. As we walked along the cresting river on roads now closed to traffic, we began to get a sense of the devastation that was about to hit.

It didn't take long for that to happen. A bordering neighborhood, Sunnyside, was the first to be forced to evacuate a few hours later. Soon after, much of our neighborhood, Hillhurst, lost all power. Friends who lived just a few blocks closer to the river came to spend the night, laden with all the food in their now-dormant refrigerator. Very quickly, walks around the block weren't curiosity-driven events, but cheerless assessments of how much longer we might have before being forced away ourselves.

As expected, an evacuation alert for our block was soon posted, as the zone just south of us was evacuated. But luckily the river began to subside before we had to leave our home.

- APPRECIATION OF COMPLEXITY: When disasters happen, victims' worlds often seem to close in. Pre-occupied with potential losses, and perhaps even consumed with just staying alive, it would be strange for them to be thinking about much else. ... That said, failing to consider some of the bigger issues can amplify problems. What other considerations might have been appropriate for the authors of this narrative?

- ATTUNEMENT TO COMPLICITY: Notice how the narrative is written in a tone of "This is happening to us." The narrators are observers and victims. There is no sense of agency or complicity. That's natural. People are likely to feel powerless and even desperate in such circumstances. That said, how might such narratives be rewritten to acknowledge greater senses of agency and complicity?

application, method, and reception that are highlighted in our chapter titles:

1 – **STEM** ((disciplinarity) transdisciplinating)
2 – **Learning** ((acquisition) participating)
3 – **Mathematics** ((calculation) modeling)
4 – **Technology** ((usage) designing)
5 – **Engineering** ((application) innovating)
6 – **Science** ((method) inquiring)
7 – **STEM Education** ((reception) contributing)

However, as we have argued, society has come to a place where those emphases are no longer sufficient. So far we have phrased this shift in terms of elaborations toward transdisciplinating, participating, modeling, designing, innovating, inquiring, and contributing. But we might just as well have phrased the evolution in terms of a realization that science, technology, engineering, and mathematics are humanities. That is, they are ways into understanding the human situation as subject to the constraints of the universe we inhabit. In Dewey's terms, they are means of appreciating "the participation of the individual in the social consciousness of the race."

So what might it mean for education to take seriously the assertion that those disciplines traditionally associated with the sciences should be appreciated as humanities rather than being defined in contradistinction to the humanities?

It is perhaps appropriate to re-mention at this point that John Dewey was the principal author of the "inquiry method." This mode of educational engagement is all about taking advantage of students' situations to catalyze their learning. Inquiry isn't about invented contexts or external motivators; it is, rather, about careful framing of the world that learners already inhabit. It is about orienting attentions, highlighting what might have gone unnoticed, offering new ways of making sense, and proposing relations among the previously disconnected. All of these activities demand the active participation of the learner, who must attend, notice, make sense, and relate in a mode of learning that is so much more than "receiving."

The sad reality is that very few classrooms reveal

The cottonwood is one of the major tree species in southern Alberta, particularly in the areas struck by the 2013 flood.

It turns out that this species requires floods to propagate, and so a highly effective mitigation scheme could potentially alter the entire ecology of the region ... perhaps creating more problems than it solves. This consideration is just one among literally hundreds for policy makers and engineers as they examine ways to mitigate future flood damage.

their grander situation. To demonstrate this point, imagine if you were asked to identify the location of a random North American classroom based on images of the room. It's likely there'd be flags and proclamations pinned to the walls that would give strong clues, but in absence of those, you probably wouldn't be able to tell if the room were in the Yukon or in California. To boot, if there were additional clues in the texts on the shelves or student work fixed to the walls, those clues would almost certainly be unrelated to STEM Education. The artifacts around mathematics and science would refuse to reveal anything about the location.

But that needn't be the case. Consider once again the contrasts between the reports of the Calgary flood presented in this chapter's opening news report and the subsequent anecdotes in the "Consolidating Key Points" sections. Following Dewey's admonition, it is possible to frame STEM Education in terms of "the demands of the social situations" in which learners find themselves.

We would add, of course, "the demands of the ecological situations" to Dewey's emphasis on the social – an elaboration that has imposed itself over the past half century. Beyond thinking about "the participation of the individual in the social consciousness of the race," educators are now called to think about the participation of the individual in the ecology of the planet. Such demands simply cannot be accomplished by delivering the facts to desk-bound recipients in nondescript, generic school rooms. Schooling, to be truly educational, must reveal itself for where it is happening – and this is as true of the STEM disciplines as it is of social studies, language learning, and physical education.

From a geological perspective, the river basin changed in almost a blink of an eye. Sediments on the erosional bank of the meandering river were swiftly swept away. Rapid gravel deposition enlarged several existing islands. The direct relationship between grain size transport and water flow was observable. Fast water moved boulders and changed the topography. It was astonishing to witness the dramatic changes to the river system: a geological event.

To make this point in specific relation to the 2013 flood in southern Alberta, consider some of the immediate and obvious ties to STEM domains:

- Geology – e.g., real-time geomorphology;
- Physical geography – e.g., a changed river basin, with new paths carved and old paths "abandoned";
- Meteorology – e.g., a coincidence of uncommon events, producing not only unusual weather patterns, but massive and catastrophic ones.

Extending the discussion a little further, some immediate topics of consideration in the social sciences include the following:

- Human geography – e.g., why humans tend to settle along waterways … and cautions they should take in doing so;
- Forestry – e.g., the role played by lumber production, as land stripped of trees holds less water and allows the sun to melt the snow faster;
- Economics – e.g., weighing the cost of solutions against the cost of no solutions.

On the last of these points, this particular environmental event didn't leave citizens of Alberta with the choice of inaction. A response was necessary, and this is where domains within engineering are most often mentioned. For example:

- Structural and civil engineering – e.g., locating, designing, and constructing dams, channels, and other structures to contain water and mitigate water damage;
- Urban planning – e.g., rethinking patterns of settlement and movement, to minimize impact next time around.

Across these possibilities, there are ample opportunities to engage in mathematics (e.g., consider the volumes of water involved, or the many aspects that lend themselves to dynamic modeling), biology (e.g., impacts on river ecology, or the role of forests in ecosystemic health), physics (e.g., velocity, acceleration, force), and other traditional branches of school science.

In brief, there was no shortage of entry points to inquiry. Yet, as noted earlier, if there were such inquiries in local schools, news of them didn't reach our ears. Rather than being seen as an opportunity to situate mathematics and science education, the flood was more often met as a massive interruption to schooling.

It's not easy to do cost–benefit analyses on flood mitigation strategies, partly because there is limited information on effectiveness and returns on investments. Moreover, such details can vary dramatically from one setting to another.

These frustrations are matched by the urgency of figuring things out. Flood disaster impacts are growing, amplified by the fact that populations continue to shift to urban settings.

Interestingly, putting things "back as they were" – by, e.g., restoring flood plains – can have consistent positive results (Hawley, Moench & Sabbag, 2012) … but the strategy can crash against intense desires for riverfront properties.

"school as a form of community life"

"[M]uch of present education fails because it neglects [the] fundamental principle of the school as a form of community life. It conceives the school as a place where certain information is to be given, where certain lessons are to be learned, or where certain habits are to be formed. The value of these is conceived as lying largely in the remote future; the child must do these things for the sake of something else he [sic] is to do; they are mere preparation. As a result they do not become a part of the life experience of the child and so are not truly educative."

Dewey's commentary was sparked, in part, by the strong themes of standardization and regulation that defined North American schools at the time. He saw them as stifling of the human spirit, as damaging to natural inclinations toward inquiry, and, ultimately,

---

Consolidating Key Points

Located on the 13-acre St. George's Island in the Bow River, the Calgary Zoo was hit hard by the flood. With only 10 hours for evacuation, plans were made by prioritizing animals in low-lying areas, ones unable to retreat and ones that were potentially dangerous if they escaped.

The tiger enclosure was at risk. Tranquilizing the six tigers with blow guns was challenging. As each tiger went down, the other tigers became more agitated. After a tiger was anesthetized, the zookeepers waited 15 minutes, put it on a tarp, dragged it into a crate, ensured its airway was clear and moved the crate to a safe location.

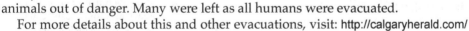

In just under 10 hours, the zoo staff moved 158 animals out of danger. Many were left as all humans were evacuated.

For more details about this and other evacuations, visit: http://calgaryherald.com/ news/local-news/ flood-at-the-calgary-zoo-the-inside-story?__lsa=aeaa-a5bc.

- APPRECIATION OF COMPLEXITY: In contrast to the previous narrative, about water levels creeping up to homes, this emergency demanded an immediate and focused response. As extreme weather events become more frequent and intense, what sorts of considerations might help to mitigate such emergencies?

- ATTUNEMENT TO COMPLICITY: The issue of the flood aside, the phenomenon of "zoo" raises a great range of issues, especially around popular perceptions of the relationships between humanity and other species. Metaphors of stewards, masters, and owners are pervasive in English. What sorts of windows does this event offer into the perceptions on humanity's place in and relationship to the rest of the world? In turn, how might the cultural phenomenon of "zoo" be related to the flood event?

as fragmenting of society. For Dewey, these structures robbed the individual of senses of agency and autonomy – and, in the process, they undermined active participation. To be honest, we find it more than a little depressing to realize that Dewey's assertions and admonitions are still current and urgent, some 120 years after they were first published.

But, to be fair, it's not that such commentary has been ignored by schools. On the contrary, over the past century, public schooling has responded with emphases on social studies, life planning, current events, and other engagements with real-world and real-time happenings. We would argue that the major reason that Dewey's admonition still feels current is not that "education" is unresponsive, but that "STEM Education" hasn't responded sufficiently.

With that point in mind, we asked ourselves how we might, as educators, "bring the flood into our classrooms." For us, this consideration starts with the reminder that the engines of inquiry are learners' natural curiosity and playfulness. After all, what child doesn't love to splash through puddles? Which youngster hasn't been fascinated by the trickles of water that run down the street after rains or during melt-offs? Who hasn't been fascinated by a river overflowing its banks?

Now consider that a puddle isn't just a basin filled with water. It's actually a window into the ground that surrounds it. If that ground is saturated, the puddle will persist. If the ground is level, the water likely won't be moving quickly and may be prone to stagnation. And so on. Similarly, the curbside trickle of water after a storm isn't just a temporary stream. It's a living demonstration of and (often irresistible) invitation to experiment with stream paths, dams, object buoyancies, flow rates, and such. That is, puddles and trickles are hosts of inquiries waiting to happen.

In other words, it's not particularly difficult to imagine possible locations for engaged STEM-oriented inquiry that might be triggered by local events. Prominent among the educator's responsibilities here are the introductions of constraints and structures that might amplify noticing, enable questioning, facilitate investigation, and support application and development

Historically, waterways (especially flood plains) were where people built and settled – but not for the view. Rather, the lures included proximity to fresh water, fertile soils, and flat landscapes, as well as ready access to a major means of transportation.

Many urban centers, built on a flood plain, are at risk of flooding. The major flood of the North Saskatchewan River in Edmonton in 1915 (42 feet above average) caused 2000 people to lose their homes. At huge cost, the city prohibited rebuilding on the flood plain. The result wasn't just better flood readiness; Edmontonians enjoy extensive natural pathways along the river valley.

of conceptual understandings. This point is brought home to us regularly when we visit a local science center. Almost always, the most popular exhibit is an interactive "flow table" in which a fluctuating stream of water runs over and through different forms. Observers of all ages are invited to play with those forms – to erect dams, to alter deltas, and so on. Whenever we're at the science center, young children and mature

---

Consolidating Key Points

Most of the media attention for the flood focused on the cities and towns of Calgary, Canmore, and High River. Arguably, however, the community most impacted was that of the Siksika First Nation. Many were evacuated. More than 250 houses were damaged or destroyed, ultimately leaving 1000 people homeless.

For several days, most of us were completely unaware of the plight experienced by our First Nations neighbors. In fact, when the first details trickled in, they weren't about the community, but damages to the Hidden Valley Resort, a popular destination at Siksika. It was much later that we heard the news that the Stoney Nakoda Nation was also devastated by the flood. Differing responsibilities between the municipal, provincial, and federal governments had left those communities in disrepair. By 2015 when 92% of residential flood claims had been addressed, only 79 out of 557 damaged homes on the Nakoda Stoney Nation were repaired (14%).

- APPRECIATION OF COMPLEXITY: The phrase "natural disaster" is misleading in this case. This narrative highlights some of the social, cultural, institutional, political, economic, and historic elements that contributed to the devastating consequences of the flood. How might such topics fit into a STEM course? How are they about science, technology, engineering, and mathematics?

- ATTUNEMENT TO COMPLICITY: For us, there's a subtle and disturbing connection between this narrative and the previous one about the Calgary Zoo. In both instances, during the disaster, we were oblivious to the situations of beings positioned as "other," whether implicitly or explicitly. It's a shame that it took a natural disaster to raise the issue for us and so many around us. How might educators help people become more mindful of "others" and the habits we use to distinguish "other" … without the impactful prompts of such unfortunate circumstances?

adults alike are immersed in playing and learning at the table. This "simple" demonstration table reveals that there are abundant entry points for inquiry for all ages around matters of water flowing over the Earth's surface – let alone the manifold possibilities that explode around massive floods in the real world outside one's classroom.

These moments remind us that the opposite of "play" isn't "work," since these learners typically appear to be putting forth considerable effort in their time-consuming, focus-demanding study of whatever it is they're playing with. Rather than "work," then, the opposite of "play" is "stillness," "inflexibility," "inaction," or "boredom" – more concisely, non-movement – precisely what is so often encountered in math and science class, where learners "do not become a part of the life experience ... and so are not truly educative."

Summing up

We end our discussion with one more provocation from Dewey:

> "[E]ducation is the fundamental method of social progress and reform."

Once again, we would extend Dewey's focus on the social to include the ecological. For us, education is the fundamental method of social and ecological progress and reform.

That is, education is not an inert or benign cultural exercise.

That's hardly news, of course. Throughout its history in the western world, formal education has overwhelmingly been framed in terms of one group's efforts to have all other groups interpret the world as they do. That notion applies to more than schooling. Governing parties, health agencies, multinational corporations, and other organizations rarely shy away from using the word *education* to refer to their initiatives to sway public opinion.

But Dewey was signaling a different conception of education in his description. He was pointing to an education that wasn't about advancing a specific

Much of the economic "damage" of the Calgary flood came in the form of inconvenience. Flooding in the downtown area triggered power outages and prevented many from going to work for several days after the water receded.

Even the city's major annual festival, the Calgary Stampede, was threatened when major parts of its venue, including its show arena, were submerged.

perspective or maintaining established knowledge and practices.

In the domain of the social for example, this is an education that isn't about preparing people for adult life or the world of paid labor. Rather than seeking to anticipate or determine the future, this is an education that's about keeping open each learner's horizon of possibility. In terms of STEM domains specifically, the point of this education is not to produce technologically literate adults who can step into the yawning gaps of an increasingly digitized work world. The point, rather, is to afford choice for each citizen. One needn't pursue a STEM-related career, but one shouldn't be denied the choice because of a poor STEM Education.

As for the domain of the ecological, STEM Education is not about just facts and skills, but about being engaged and attentive in an open, informed manner – a point that might be illustrated with the example of the Calgary flood. Since that actual event, residents of the region have been presented with proposal after proposal for mitigating future flood damage. Unfortunately, those suggestions are falling on the ears of a public that has been poorly educated in STEM. In consequence, reactions tend to be based on near-sighted issues such as "how much it costs" or "how it affects me," instead of being focused on more global considerations such as impact on "others" and the local ecology.

In brief, most people don't know how to contribute to the conversation. Concerns tend to land on the present moment, the local context, and the personal cost, rather than on future consequences, the broader ecosystem, and impacts on other individuals and communities. Few pause to seek out additional facts, to pose necessary questions, to consider wider conversations.

The margin notes and the "Consolidating Key Points" boxes in this chapter were offered in part to trouble this tendency. They point to additional considerations, unintended consequences, and other elements that present windows into the true complexity of the situation. But they represent just a small sampling of the full spectrum of social and environmental considerations. While it would be impossible to catalog them all, it is important to embrace their existence.

Tshering Tobgay's TED Talk, "This country isn't just carbon neutral – it's carbon negative" [https://www.ted.com/talks/tshering_tobgay_this_country_isn_t_just_carbon_neutral_it_s_carbon_negative] **offers provocative insights into current debates about climate change. Even though Tobgay's home country of Bhutan absorbs more carbon than it emits, it must deal with flooding as glaciers melt at unprecedented rates.**

Therein lies a critical feature of a strong STEM Education – which doesn't prepare a learner by providing the answers, but enables the learner to engage with life's questions. It is not about implementing plans, but of iterative responsiveness as one acts in an informed manner, assesses the consequences of those actions, and revises those actions on the basis of emergent information.

In this way, education is not about imposing one group's ways of seeing the world onto another group. It is about expanding the space of the possible by exploring the current space of possibilities. It is genuinely an education that proceeds on the belief that every individual contributes to the world, and so to the extent possible that contribution should be informed and mindful. Education should indeed be the fundamental method of social and ecological progress and reform.

Contributing Challenges

1. Read all of John Dewey's "My Pedagogic Creed," taking note of the lines that resonate and the lines that grate. Revise them to fit with your own emerging creed on STEM Education.

2. Consider using the Calgary flood (or a similar event that might be more relevant to your situation) as a focus to think through what it means to design an inquiry. Where would you start? (We offered several possible entry points, but there are many others.) How might you prepare to hear student reactions and to layer in additional questions or information that might channel discussions toward a viable and valuable inquiry? What might you insert as prompts or nudges to span STEM domains?

3. As developed in Chapter 2, words matter, especially when it comes to the ways that educators talk about knowing and learning. Vocabularies channel attentions and frame interpretations. That is, explicit descriptions have implicit prescriptions.

   Revisit the tables presented in Chapter 2, in which we delved into clusters of metaphors for knowledge, learning, learners, and education that are associated with different theories of learning. When we assembled those tables, we deliberately left out metaphors for teaching ... so that we could ask you to participate in the following sorts of considerations: What is teaching, for you? What synonyms and descriptions of teaching spring to mind when you hear that question? How do your words you associate with "teaching" align with the different learning theories considered in Chapter 2? Are you content with those alignments?

References

Alberta Education. (1996). *Elementary science program of study*. Edmonton, AB: Government of Alberta.

Alberta Education. (2008). *Mathematics Grades 10–12 program of studies*. Edmonton, AB: Government of Alberta.

Alberta Education. (2014). *Mathematics Kindergarten to Grade 9*. Edmonton, AB: Government of Alberta.

Arellano, N. E. (2015, March 30). Why Canada has an 182,000 IT talent shortage while lots of tech professionals are out of work. *IT World Canada*. Retrieved from http://www.itworldcanada.com/article/why-canada-has-an-182000-it-talent-shortage-while-lots-of-tech-professionals-are-out-of-work/373517

Barrow, J. D. (1993). *Pi in the sky: Counting, thinking and being*. London: Penguin.

Berger, P., & Luckmann, T. (1967). *The social construction of reality: A treatise in the sociology of knowledge*. Garden City, NY: Anchor Books.

Bhasin, K. (2012). This is the difference between "invention" and "innovation." *Business Insider*. Retrieved from http://www.businessinsider.com/this-is-the-difference-between-invention-and-innovation-2012-4

Black, M. (1962). *Models and metaphors*. Ithaca: Cornell University Press.

Bransford, J. D., Brown, A. L., & Cocking, R. R. (1999). *How people learn: Brain, mind, experience and school*. Washington, DC: National Academy Press.

Brown, A. L. (1992). Design experiments: Theoretical and methodological challenges in creating complex interventions in classroom settings. *The Journal of the Learning Sciences, 2*(2), 141–178.

Bruner, J. S. (1960). *The process of education*. Cambridge, MA: Harvard University Press.

Bruner, J. (1966). *Toward a theory of instruction*. Cambridge, MA: Harvard University Press.

Carey, B. (2014). H*ow we learn: The surprising truth about when, where, and why it happens.* New York: Random House Publishing Group.

Choi, B. C. K., & Pak, A. W. P. (2006). Multidisciplinarity, interdisciplinarity and transdisciplinarity in health research, services, education and policy. *Clinical and Investigative Medicine. Medecine Clinique et Experimentale, 29*(6), 351–364.

Clendenin, B. (2014, July 31). Canada's IT labour shortage: Challenges and opportunities. *IT Business.* Retrieved from http://www.itbusiness.ca/blog/canadas-it-labour-shortage-challenges-and-opportunities/50250

Coker, R. (2001). *Distinguishing science and pseudoscience.* Retrieved June 25, 2017, from https://www.quackwatch.org/01QuackeryRelatedTopics/pseudo.html

Cuban, L. (2003). *Oversold and underused: Computers in the classroom.* Cambridge, MA: Harvard University Press.

Davis, B., & Renert, M. (2014). *The math teachers know: Profound understandings of emergent mathematics.* New York: Routledge.

Davis, B., Sumara, D., & Luce-Kapler, R. (2015). *Engaging minds: Cultures of education and practices of teaching* (3rd edn.). New York: Routledge.

DeMott, B. (1962). The math wars. *American Scholar, 31,* 296–310.

Dewey, J. (1897). My pedagogic creed. *School Journal, 54,* 77–80.

Dumont, H., Istance, D., & Benevides, F. (2010). *The nature of learning: Using research to inspire practice.* Paris: OECD Publishing. Retrieved from https://www.oecd.org/edu/ceri/50300814.pdf

Dweck, C. S. (2007). *Mindset: The new psychology of success.* New York: Random House Publishing Group.

Friesen, S. (2009). *What did you do in school today? Teaching effectiveness: A framework and rubric.* Toronto, ON: Canadian Education Association.

Geary, J. (2011). *I is an other: The secret life of metaphor and how it shapes the way we see the world.* New York: Harper Collins.

Hawley, K., Moench, M, & Sabbag, L. (2012). *Understanding the economics of flood risk reduction: A preliminary analysis.* Boulder, CO: Institute for Social and Environmental Trasition-International.

Hiebert, J., & Wearne, D. (1986). Procedures over concepts: The acquisition of decimal number knowledge. In J. Hiebert (Ed.), *Conceptual and procedural knowledge: The case of mathematics* (pp. 199–223). Hillsdale, NJ: Lawrence Erlbaum.

Kelly, K. (2010). *What technology wants.* New York: Penguin.

Lakoff, G., & Johnson, M. (1999). *Philosophy in the flesh: The embodied mind & its challenge to western thought.* New York: Basic Books.

Lakoff, G., & Núñez, R. (2000). *Where mathematics comes from: How the embodied mind brings mathematics into being.* New York: Basic Books.

Lave, J., & Wenger, E. (1991). *Situated learning: Legitimate peripheral participation.* Cambridge, UK: Cambridge University Press.

Merleau-Ponty, M. (1962). *The phenomenology of perception.* London: Routledge and Kegan Paul.

National Council of Teachers of Mathematics. (1989). *Curriculum and evaluation standards for school mathematics.* Reston, VA: National Council of Teachers of Mathematics.

OECD. (2013). *Skills for the digital economy (OECD skills strategy spotlight better skills, better jobs, better lives)* (p. 4). Paris, France: Organisation for Economic Co-operation and Development. Retrieved from http://skills.oecd.org/developskills/documents/Skills_for_the_Digital_Economy_SSS4.pdf

OECD. (2015). *Students, computers and learning: Making the connections.* Paris, France: OECD Publishing. Retrieved from http://www.oecd-ilibrary.org/education/students-computers-and-learning_9789264239555-en

Piaget, J. (1954). Language and thought from a genetic perspective. *Acta Psychologica, 10,* 51–60. https://doi.org/10.1016/0001-6918(54)90004-9

Rudolph, J.L. (2005). Epistemology for the masses: The origins of the "scientific method" in American schools. *History of Education Quarterly, 45*(2), 341–376.

Scardamalia, M., & Bereiter, C. (2006). Knowledge building: Theory, pedagogy, and technology. In R. K. Sawyer (Ed.), *The Cambridge handbook of the learning sciences* (1st ed., pp. 97–119). New York: Cambridge University Press.

Scardamalia, M., & Bereiter, C. (2014). Knowledge building and knowledge creation: Theory, pedagogy and technology. In R. K. Sawyer (Ed.), *The Cambridge handbook of the learning sciences* (2nd ed., pp. 397–417). New York: Cambridge University Press.

Schubert, W. H. (1986). *Curriculum: Perspective, paradigm, and possibility.* London, UK: Macmillan Publishing Company.

Shulman, L. S. (1986). Those who understand: Knowledge growth in teaching. *Educational Researcher, 15,* 4–14.

Shulman, L. S. (1987). Knowledge and teaching: Foundations of the new reform. *Harvard Educational Review, 57*(1), 1–22.

Sfard, A. (1998). On two metaphors for learning and the dangers of choosing just one. *Educational Researcher, 27*(2), 4–13. https://doi.org/10.3102/0013189X027002004

Skinner, B. F. (1950). Are theories of learning necessary? *Psychological Review, 57*, 193–216.

Thorndike, E. L. (1931). *Human learning*. New York: Century Company.

Weiner, J., Simpson, J. A., & Proffitt, M. (1993). *Oxford English Dictionary*. Oxford, UK: Oxford University Press.

Willingham, D. (2009). *Why don't students like school? A cognitive scientist answers questions about how the mind works and what it means for the classroom*. New York: Jossey-Bass.

Zemplén, G. Á. (2009). Putting sociology first – reconsidering the role of the social in "nature of science" education. *Science & Education, 18*(5), 525–559. https://doi.org/10.1007/s11191-007-9125-3

Acknowledgments

We would like to recognize those teachers, researchers, and scholars who have labored to interrupt the assumptions and norms that frame popular understandings of education and teaching. Only a handful of these persons could be mentioned in the text, but we acknowledge our work is only made possible by theirs.

More locally, we are indebted to Dana Poscente, Michael Poscente, and Sophia Poscente for their many layers of proofreading and critique. We also acknowledge the contributions of instructors and students of EDUC 427 ("STEM Education"), who test-ran previous iterations of this book over the past several years.

The hand-drawn images throughout the book were done by Wayne Eng. We (Brent, Krista, and Sharon) were responsible for the digital drawings of the models in Chapters 2, 5, and 6, and the instantiations of sines, tangents, and multiplication in Chapter 3. Photographs in Chapters 3, 5, and 6 are courtesy of the Galileo Network (University of Calgary). Images in Chapter 4 are courtesy of Krista Francis. Credits for photographs in Chapter 7 are as follows:

pp. 111, 112, 113: Ryan L. C. Quan [CC BY-SA 3.0 (https://creativecommons.org/licenses/by-sa/3.0)], from Wikimedia Commons [https://commons.wikimedia.org/wiki/File:East_Village_Calgary_Flood_2013.jpg; https://commons.wikimedia.org/wiki/File:Riverfront_Ave_Calgary_Flood_2013.jpg; https://commons.wikimedia.org/wiki/File:Centre_Street_Bridge_Calgary_Flood_2013.jpg]

p. 114: Shannon [GFDL (http://www.gnu.org/copyleft/fdl.html) or CC BY-SA 4.0 (https://creativecommons.org/licenses/by-sa/4.0)], via Wikimedia Commons [https://commons.wikimedia.org/wiki/File:Bowrivermap.jpg]

p. 117: Krista Francis

p. 119: Dave Bloggs [CC BY 2.0 (https://creativecommons.org/licenses/by/2.0)], via Wikimedia Commons [https://commons.wikimedia.org/wiki/File:Elbow_falls_Kananaskis_Alberta_Canada_(26217023220).jpg]

p. 120: Samsamcat [Public domain, CC0 or Public domain], via Wikimedia Commons [https://commons.wikimedia.org/wiki/File:2013_Glenmore_Res-
ervoir_flooding.jpg]

p. 121: Alexander Leisser [CC BY-SA 4.0 (https://creativecommons.org/licenses/
by-sa/4.0)], from Wikimedia Commons [https://commons.wikimedia.org/wiki/
File:Tiger_Zoo_Vienna.jpg]

p. 122: Blv0921 [CC BY-SA 4.0 (https://creativecommons.org/licenses/by-
sa/4.0)], from Wikimedia Commons [https://commons.wikimedia.org/wiki/
File:Bassano_Dam_June_23,_2013.jpg]

p. 123: Samsamcat [GFDL (http://www.gnu.org/copyleft/fdl.html) or CC BY-SA
3.0 (https://creativecommons.org/licenses/by-sa/3.0)], via Wikimedia Commons [https://commons.wikimedia.org/wiki/File:Bridge_on_Siksika_nation_destroyed_
by_flood.jpg]

p. 124: Sean Esopenko [CC BY-SA 2.0 (https://creativecommons.org/licenses/
by-sa/2.0)], via Wikimedia Commons [https://commons.wikimedia.org/wiki/
File:Flood_Waters_Rushing_Past_Downtown,_Calgary_June_2013.jpg]

p. 125: Jean-Marie Hullot [CC BY-SA 2.0 (https://creativecommons.org/licenses/
by-sa/2.0)], via Wikimedia Commons [https://commons.wikimedia.org/wiki/
File:Cloudhidden,_whereabouts_unknown_(Paro,_Bhutan).jpg]

Index